Cheyenne Major Constituent Order

Volume Editors

Marilyn Mayers
Rhonda Hartell
Laurie Nelson

Production Staff

Laurie Nelson, Production Manager
Judy Benjamin, Compositor
Jennifer Lonas, Compositor
Hazel Shorey, Graphic Artist

Cheyenne Major Constituent Order

Elena M. Leman

A Publication of
The Summer Institute of Linguistics

©1999 by the Summer Institute of Linguistics, Inc.
Library of Congress Catalog No: 97-69390
ISBN: 1-55671-015-1

Printed in the United States of America
All Rights Reserved

O9 08 07 06 05 04 03 02 01 00   10 9 8 7 6 5 4 3 2 1

No part of this publication may be reproduced, stored in a retrieval system, or transmitted in any form or by any means—electronic, mechanical, photocopy, recording, or otherwise—without the express permission of the Summer Institute of Linguistics, with the exception of brief excerpts in journal articles or reviews.

Copies of this and other publications of the Summer Institute of Linguistics may be obtained from

International Academic Bookstore
Summer Institute of Linguistics
7500 W. Camp Wisdom Rd.
Dallas, TX 75236-5699

Voice: 972-708-7404
Fax: 972-708-7433
Email: academic_books@sil.org
Internet: http://www.sil.org

Contents

Acknowledgments vii
Abbreviations ix
1. Introduction 1
2. Grammatical Overview 5
   2.1 Obviation 5
   2.2 Verb inflection 6
   2.3 Pronominal prefixes and inverse markers 7
   2.4 Indirect object 8
3. A Typological Perspective 11
   3.1 Syntactic role and constituent order. 11
   3.2 Semantic role and constituent order. 13
   3.3 Animacy and constituent order 16
   3.4 First mention and constituent order. 17
   3.5 Tomlin's Theme First Principle 22
   3.6 Tomlin's Animated First Principle. 32
   3.7 Payne's combinations of factors. 35
   3.8 Other combinations 36
4. Newsworthy First 37
   4.1 Newsworthy contrasted with other linguistic terms. . 38
   4.2 Tests for Mithun's newsworthy first principle . . . 41
   4.3 Other support for newsworthy first 48
   4.4 Cognitive support for the hypothesis 51

5. Experimental Approach to Newsworthy First. 53
   5.1 Introduction to the experiment 53
   5.2 On-line video narration 54
6. Results of the Experiment and Newsworthy First 63
7. Conclusion 77
Appendix A. Cumulative Referential Density in Cheyenne 79
Appendix B. Diary of Video Experiment Process 83
Appendix C. Samples of Cheyenne Texts 87
References. 91

Acknowledgments

This book is based on my thesis which fulfilled the requirements for obtaining my master's degree at the University of Oregon in 1991. I am indebted to my advisor, Professor Russell Tomlin, for his assistance in the preparation of the thesis. In addition, special thanks are due to my husband, Wayne Leman, whose help with the Cheyenne language and computer expertise were invaluable throughout the research and preparation that went into this manuscript. I would like to thank those who helped me prepare this manuscript for publication. Special thanks are also due to each of the Cheyenne people who assisted me in my experimental investigation of their language. My deepest gratitude is to God, without whom this manuscript could not have been completed.

Abbreviations

1	first person
1PL	first person plural
1PS	first person possessor
2	second person
2PS	second person possessor
3	third person
3PL	third person plural
3PS	third person possessor
å	voiceless *a*
AFP	Animated First Principle
Ag	agent
AL, EA, EK, GO, IR, LF, TR	Cheyenne speakers who participated in the on-line video narration experiment
AK, DL	Cheyenne speakers who contributed to the research
AN	animate
AI	animate subject, intransitive verb
ATTR	attributive mode (generally, hearsay)
CATAPH	cataphoric reference (pointing forward)
CD	communicative dynamism
CJT	conjunct
CRD	cumulative referential density
DEL^IMP	delayed imperative
Dem	demonstrative
DIM	diminutive

DIR	direct (i.e., the person indicated in the prefix of a transitive verb is the actor)
DUB	dubitative mode
e̊	voiceless *e*
EP	Elena's paragraph breaks
excl	exclusive
FM	first mention
FUT	future
HABIT	habitual aspect
ID	identifiable
II	inanimate subject, intransitive verb
IMP	imperative
IMPERS	impersonal
INAN	inanimate
INT	intentive (to do with the purpose of)
INV	inverse (i.e., the person indicated in the prefix of a transitive verb is the recipient of the action)
LOC	locative
N	noun
NEG	negative
NFM	nonfirst mention
NI	nonidentifiable
NP	noun phrase
O	object
o̊	voiceless *o*
OBL	oblique
OBV	obviative/obviated
PL	plural
PRET	preterit mode
PROHIB	prohibitive
PROX	proximate
PST	past tense
PSV	passive
Pt	patient
RECIP	reciprocal
RD	referential density
REFL	reflexive
S	subject
š	esh
TA	transitive verb, animate object
TFP	Theme First Principle
TI	transitive verb, inanimate object

Abbreviations

V	verb
VOB	Verb Object Bonding Principle
VP	verb phrase
WP	Wayne's paragraph breaks
x	unspecified

\>   The element to the left of this sign is more thematic than the element to the right; or the element to the left of the sign is higher on the hierarchy in question than the element to the right of the sign.

^   Links two or more words in the English gloss when the translation of a single vernacular word requires more than one English word.

-     Indicates morpheme breaks in a Cheyenne word and in the corresponding English gloss.

1
Introduction

Cheyenne is a member of the Algonquian language family and is spoken by approximately two thousand people, most of whom live in Oklahoma and southeastern Montana. Only a few lexical items distinguish the speech of the Montana Cheyenne from that of the Oklahoma Cheyenne.

In the corpus of Cheyenne narrative texts studied for this research, all possible combinations of order of the major constituents, subject (S), verb (V), and object (O), occur, i.e., SVO, SOV, VOS, VSO, OVS, and OSV. These are illustrated in examples (1)–(6) below.[1] Since languages are limited in the number of linguistic devices they can use in communication, it is likely that Cheyennes use a variation of constituent order to communicate information not otherwise stated outright. This book explores the factors which influence the order of major constituents in Cheyenne narrative.

---

[1]Some of these examples are taken from Leman 1980 with page and clause number indicated; some are from the on-line video narrations done by Cheyenne speakers AL and IR. Linguistic labels used in chapter 1, including S, V, and O, will be rigorously defined in chapter 3.

2   Cheyenne Major Constituent Order

(1) Leman 1980:38.4 SVO

S	V	O
na'ęstse	é-s-ta-éve-ame-måheénenán-ŏ-hoon-ŏtse	kęhamaxę̂-stse
one	3-PST-away-about-along-gather-INAN-PRET-PL	stick-PL[2]

One was gathering firewood.

(2) AL Chicken story, second telling, clause 25 SOV

S	O	V
tá'tóhe hetane	he-stohkǒxe	é-ta-éva-ame-no'e-ohtse
that^AN man	3PS-ax	3-away-back-along-with-go

That man carries his ax back.

(3) Leman 1980:57.69 VOS

V

mó-me'-ée-hé-heškévo'-óht-a
DUB-would-about-INT-nick-by^mouth-INAN

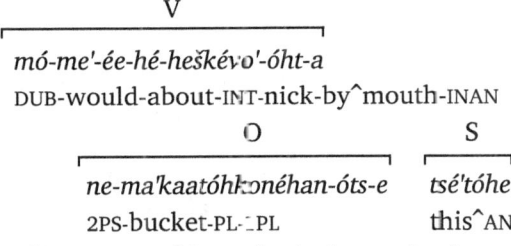

O	S
ne-ma'kaatóhkonéhan-óts-e	tsé'tóhe
2PS-bucket-PL-PL	this^AN

This one would surely drain our buckets.

(4) Leman 1980:45.29 VSO

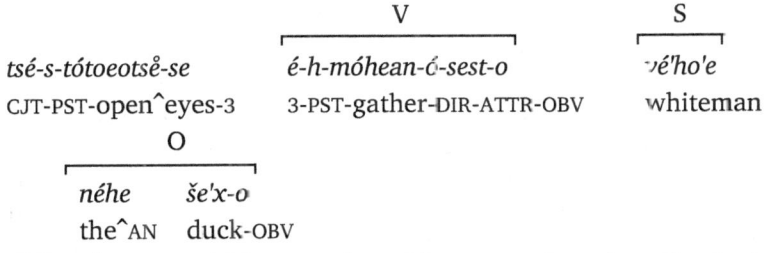

	V	S
tsé-s-tótoeotsę̂-se	é-h-móhean-ó-sest-o	vé'ho'e
CJT-PST-open^eyes-3	3-PST-gather-DIR-ATTR-OBV	whiteman

O
néhe   še'x-o
the^AN duck-OBV

When he opened his eyes, the whiteman gathered up the ducks

---

[2]Throughout the book, the literal gloss line gives enough information for the purpose of constituent order investigation but does not give a complete morpheme-by-morpheme translation.

Introduction

(5) IR Chicken story, first telling, clause 3 OVS

O	V	S
kåhamaxê-stse	é-ta-aseotsêstsé-nê-hoon-ôtse	néhe he'e
stick-PL	3-away-carry^INAN-INAN-PRET-PL	the^AN woman

That woman carried the sticks.

(6) IR Chicken story, third telling, clause 9 OSV

	O	S
naa	kåhamaxê-stse	néhe he'e
and	stick-PL	the^AN woman

V

é-ta-móhe-an-a-n-ôtse
3-away-gather-by^hand-INAN-INAN-PL

And that woman gathered up the sticks.

The initial study was done using ten texts by Jeanette Howlingcrane which were published in Leman 1980. Nine of these are traditional stories and one is a brief first-person narrative. Clauses[3] which preceded or followed a direct quotation, such as example (7), were not included in the study since the verb in this type of clause is almost always clause-initial.

(7) Leman 1980:26.20

é-x-het-ae-hoon-o	pe'-o
3-PST-say-INV-PRET-OBV	nighthawk-OBV

The nighthawk told her.

The number of clauses studied from the written texts was 656. Only five of these clauses had two noun phrases whose syntactic roles differed from each other. These five clauses exhibited two of the six possible major constituent orders. Except for one text, all of the Howlingcrane texts are Cheyenne stories which are well-known to Cheyennes as part of their folklore. Such familiarity is likely to produce gaps in the story. The speaker and hearer have no difficulty filling in the gap but a non-Cheyenne analyst may not even be aware there is a gap or does not know how to fill it in. To

---

[3]CLAUSE is defined as an independent verb with its constituents.

avoid the problem of shared knowledge gaps, the second part of the research consisted of the elicitation and analysis of Cheyenne narrations of two "wordless" videos. The video-elicited data also provided standardized texts in which each telling narrated the same story based on the same scenes in the same sequence. This facilitated grouping sentences about the same scene in the video in order to compare which major constituents were used and the order in which they occurred. The video-elicitation resulted in 21 texts ranging in length from 13 to 101 clauses, for a total of 976 clauses. There was no quoted material in this data. There were 26 clauses, containing two noun phrases of different syntactic roles, that used five out of the six logically possible constituent orders.

In chapter 2, a brief overview of Cheyenne grammar is presented. Some characteristics of the grammar that influence the analysis of constituent order are discussed.

Chapter 3 looks at constituent order from several typological points of view, examining a number of factors that may influence the placement of a noun either before or after a verb. Applying these factors to the Hoewlingcrane texts, statistical data is presented to help determine if these parameters can adequately predict constituent order in Cheyenne. For this study, the factors investigated are syntactic role, semantic role, animacy, first mention, a native speaker's ranking of participants, rank by total number of mentions in the text, or some combinations of these factors. Tomlin's (1986) Theme First Principle and Animated First Principle of basic constituent order are also discussed in their relationship to Cheyenne to determine if thematic rank or animatedness could influence the placement of a noun phrase either preverbally or postverbally. Also examined in are Payne's (1987) hypotheses on information structuring for Pima-Papago.

Chapter 4 presents a definition for newsworthy and the hypothesis that the most newsworthy major constituent occurs initially in a Cheyenne clause. It looks at Mithun's claim that for Coos, Cayuga, and Ngandi, the most newsworthy item is clause-initial. The tests that Mithun employed to demonstrate the Newsworthy First Principle in those languages are applied to the Howlingcrane texts to show that Cheyenne patterns in a similar way. Cognitive support for newsworthy first as a basis for Cheyenne major constituent order is also provided.

Chapter 5 details the procedure used to test the hypothesis. The experimental procedure involved the elicitation of Cheyenne narrations of short videotaped stories. The chapter ends with a compilation of the various Cheyenne narrations (translated into English) of one of the videos.

An analysis of narration data from the video-elicited texts is given in chapter 6. Statistics are presented which support the newsworthy first hypothesis and which account for alternate constituent order.

2
Grammatical Overview

This chapter presents some of the characteristics of Cheyenne grammar which influence the analysis of constituent order in Cheyenne narratives. Discussed are obviation, verb inflection, pronominal prefixes and inverse markers, and indirect object versus direct object.

2.1 Obviation

Cheyenne and other Algonquian languages keep track of participants in part by the use of OBVIATION, which is a grammatical marking to differentiate third-person participants. When there is only one third-person participant in a discourse segment in Cheyenne, it is marked only on the verb and is called a proximate (PROX). The proximate is the most focal participant in a discourse segment. Any other third-person participant is called an obviative (OBV), and its obviative status is marked on the verb and on the NP that represents it, if there is one (see Leman 1979:21). Examples (8) and (9) illustrate clauses with no obviatives; there is only one third-person participant.

(8) ná-vóó-m-o   hetane
     1-see-AN-3^DIR   man
     I see a man.

(9) ná-vóó-m-o   he'e
     1-see-AN-3^DIR   woman
     I see a woman.

In examples (10) and (11) there are two third-person participants. In each, one of the nouns is obligatorily marked as obviative by a suffix which has the allomorphic spelling -óho. The same suffix, here with allomorph -ho, occurs on the verb to indicate that there is an obviated third person who is the object of the action (cf. (3) and (9) which lack an obviated suffix).

(10) hetane   é-vóo-m-ó-ho⁴   he'-óho
      man   3-see-AN-3^DIR-OBV   woman-OBV
      The man saw the woman.

(11) hetan-óho   é-vóo-m-ó-ho   he'e
      man-OBV   3-see-AN-3^DIR-OBV   woman
      The woman saw the man.

2.2 Verb inflection

As with other Algonquian languages, Cheyenne has four classes of verbal inflections depending on the transitivity of the verb and the animacy of the participants. Bloomfield (1946) first described these classes as (1) AI: Animate (subject) Intransitive, (2) II: Inanimate (subject) Intransitive, (3) TA: Transitive Animate (object), and (4) TI: Transitive Inanimate (object).

For transitive verbs, the subject is animate unless a special inanimate subject suffix indicates that it is not.⁵ The respective suffixes indicate which person did the action to whom and is translated in the English gloss by using the corresponding person number. The table in (12) illustrates the four verb classes (from Leman 1979:18), here with the suffix allomorphs -ahe/-ta (AI), -a'e/-'o (II), -o (TA), and -a (TI).

Although not indicated in (12), negating a verb and pluralizing the participants support the validity of these four categories.

---

⁴Cf. the pitch contours of (8) and (10). The underlying phonemic shape of Cheyenne 'see-AN' is /-vóo-m/ and for third person it is /-ó/, in (10) and (11) as well as in (8) and (9). Pitch rules, described in Leman (1981), create the surface phonetic variations found here. Throughout this book, the Cheyenne transcriptions, including those for which morpheme breaks are indicated, are written with surface rather than underlying pitches.

⁵This suffix is not included here since it occurs infrequently, has a complicated form due to coalescence of vowels, and is not germaine to this study.

(12) Intransitive AI:AN subject   II:INAN subject

é-pȩ̊hev-ahe
3-good-AN
He is good.

é-pȩ̊hév-a'e
3-good-INAN
It is good.

é-tåhpe-ta
3-big-AN
He is big.

é-tåhpé-'o
3-big-INAN
It is big.

Transitive TA:AN subject and object   TI:AN subject, INAN object

ná-pȩ̊hév-án-o
1-good-by^hand-AN
I fixed him up.

é-pȩ̊hév-án-a
3-good-by^hand-INAN
He fixed it up.

ná-vóó-m-o
1-see^AN-3^DIR
I see him.

ná-vóó-ht-a
1-see-INAN-INAN
I see it.

2.3 Pronominal prefixes and inverse markers

There are three personal prefixes for verbs: *ná-* (first person), *né-* (second person), *é-* (third person). These are hierarchically ranked as 2 > 1 > 3 > OBV > INAN. When the higher-ranked person of a transitive verb is the syntactic subject, there is a direct relation: the subject is referenced in the prefix and the object in the suffix. If a person lower on the hierarchy acts on a higher-ranked participant, there is an inverse relationship: the higher-ranked person is referenced in the prefix, and the lower-ranked person, whether subject or object, is referenced in the suffix. The direct and inverse relationships determine the distribution of prefixes as follows: *né-* whenever second person is involved in any way; *ná-* first person when there is no second person; *é-* third person when there is no second or first. The suffixes are: *-atse* first-person subject with second-person object, *-e* first-person object with second-person subject, *-a* third-person subject with either second- or first-person object, *-o* third-person object with either second- or first-person subject, *-aa'e* third-person obviative subject with third-person object, *-ho* third-person obviative object with third-person subject. The table in (13) from Leman 1979:21–22, illustrates these direct and inverse verb markers.

(13) Direct   Inverse

   ná-vóó-m-o⁶   ná-vóo-m-a
   1-see-AN-3^DIR   1-see-AN-3^INV
   I saw him.   He saw me.

   né-vóó-m-o   né-vóo-m-a
   2-see-AN-3^DIR   2-see-AN-3^INV
   You saw him.   He saw you.

   né-vóo-m-e   né-vóo-m-åtse
   2-see-AN-1^DIR   2-see-AN-1^INV
   You saw me.   I saw you.

   né-vóo-m-e-me   né-vóo-m-atse-me
   2-see-AN-1^DIR-PL   2-see-AN-1^INV-PL
   You (PL) saw me.   I saw you (PL).

   é-voo-m-ó-ho   é-voo-m-aa'e
   3-see-AN-3^DIR-OBV   3-see-AN-OBV^INV
   He saw her (OBV).   She (OBV) saw him.

This person hierarchy is not limited to Cheyenne but occurs in other Algonquian languages as well.

2.4 Indirect object

In Cheyenne, a semantic animate dative (recipient) is syntactically treated as the direct object. This becomes apparent by examining the person hierachy outlined in §2.3 and the transitivity animacy classes described in §2.2. Note examples (14) and (15). Transitive verbs such as these index the animacy and number of the subject and object of a clause. When the object is higher on the person hierarchy than the subject, the object has prefixal control. If the indirect object in (14) *né-* 'you' were not syntactically treated as the direct object, the verb would have a

---

[6]The suffixes are glossed in an over-simplified way which is sufficient for the purposes of this discussion.

Grammatical Overview

first-person prefix *ná-* since first person is ranked higher than an inanimate plural object. But instead, it has a *né-* 'you' prefix, and the suffix *-atse* (first on second person inverse), used when the agent is lower on the hierarchy than the object. The prefix on the verb and the use of *-atse* indicate that the semantic indirect object is treated as the direct object of the verb.

(14) *né-mét-atse-me-nǒ-tse*
2-give-1^INV-PL-1PL-INAN^PL
We (excl) gave them (INAN) to you. or We (excl) gave them (INAN) to you (PL).

Example (15) is similar. If the indirect object 'me' were not syntactically treated as the direct object, the prefix of the verb would have to be *é-* (third person) because a third person is of higher rank than the inanimate 'them' (e.g., cookies). Example (15), however, uses the verbal prefix *ná-* (first person) which is ranked higher than third person and the suffix *-óe* (third-person inverse) which demonstrates that the semantic indirect object (recipient) 'me' is treated as the direct object.

(15) *ná-honóhtom-óe-n-ǒtse*
1-bake-3^INV-INAN-PL
He baked them for me.

3
A Typological Perspective

This chapter examines various factors used by linguists to explain constituent order in other languages. It looks at syntactic role, semantic role, animacy, and first mention with regard to constituent order. Also discussed are Tomlin's Theme First Principle and Animated First Principle, as well as Payne's combination of factors, and some other combinations. These factors are then applied to Cheyenne in order to determine if they can adequately describe its constituent order. The Howlingcrane texts provide the data base for this chapter.

3.1 Syntactic role and constituent order

The terms SUBJECT and OBJECT have been used and defined in various ways by linguists. Givón acknowledges the difficulty of giving a rigorous definition of these two roles and says of subject that "most languages tend to assign the discourse-pragmatic role of subject/topic to the agent in simple sentences" (1984:87). He also claims that "the subject case tends to code the most important, recurrent, continuous topic" (1984:138) while noting that subject can be used with other semantic roles such as patient-subject and dative-subject. His treatment of object includes calling it a prototypical patient-of-change and saying that it "codes the topic next in importance" to the subject.

Keenan (1976) argues for a universal definition of subject which also allows for language specific means of marking NPs. He presents a list of thirty properties which basic subjects characteristically possess. These properties fall under four categories: autonomy, case marking, semantic role, and immediate dominance. He was not able to isolate any combination of these properties which were both necessary and sufficient for a NP of any sentence in any language to be designated as the subject of a particular sentence. Instead, in a given sentence in any language, the NP with a preponderance of the subject properties will be the subject of that particular sentence.

Dixon proposes that all languages work in terms of three primitive relations which would be S (intransitive subject), A (transitive subject), and O (transitive object). He further defines a universal category "subject" as the class {A, S}. He states that "for a transitive clause with two core arguments, one will be mapped onto the A relation and the other onto the O relation" (1994:6). In such a case, potential agency distinguishes the argument mapped to A from the argument mapped to O.

Chomsky defines the subject of a sentence in formal terms as that NP immediately dominated by the sentence node. The direct object of a sentence is that NP immediately dominated by the VP node. He writes these concisely as: "Subject-of: [NP, S]" and "Direct-Object-of: [NP, VP]" (1965:71).

Foley and Van Valin assume syntactic subjects and objects and differentiate these categories from "actor" and "undergoer" (1984:29).

There has been a long tradition of regarding the object as both a structural category and a semantic category of patient/accusative. Fillmore defines object as "the entity that moves or changes or whose position or existence is in consideration" (1971:376). Relational grammarians have separated the grammatical and semantic elements of the usage of object and subject.

For a discussion of the relationship between Cheyenne Major constituent order and syntax, it is necessary to define subject, object, and verb. Following Tomlin (1986), subject is defined here in purely syntactic terms and does not include as identifying characteristics topic or theme, agent or other semantic roles, or information levels. Similarly, following Tomlin (1986) and Postal (1974), object is also defined in purely syntactic terms and does not include the semantic role of patient in its definition.

Cheyenne frequently allows clauses with no overt NP albeit with subjects and objects marked by verb affixes. Therefore, a comprehensive definition of subject and object in Cheyenne would need to account for clauses with no overt NPs. Since this is a study of constituent order, however, it is necessary to use an operational definition of subject and object derived from clauses that do have overt subject and object NPs. Such definitions refer to the direct and inverse markers on the verb and the treatment of indirect objects as direct objects presented in chapter 2.

A Typological Perspective

Operational definitions

SUBJECT: The subject is (1) that NP indexed by the initial prefix of the verb in its direct form or (2) that NP which is indexed in the appropriate verbal suffix if the verb is marked as an inverse.

OBJECT: The object is (1) that NP which is indexed by the appropriate suffix of the direct verb or (2) that NP indexed by the prefix of the verb if the verb is marked as an inverse.

VERB: The verb is the verb word composed of the verb stem and all accompanying parts (e.g., tense and manner) including prefixes and suffixes.

In the corpus used for this study, subjects are nearly equally divided in their placement either preverbally or postverbally. Objects follow the verb 81% of the time, nearly a fifth of the objects (19%) precede the verb. This nearly random distribution of subject indicates that syntactic role alone does not determine constituent order. The tables in (16) and (17) give the specific percentages of the two roles and their linear order with respect to the verb.

(16) Subject and verb order

	SV		VS		Total	
Subject	55	47%	63	53%	118	100%

(17) Object and verb order

	OV		VO		Total	
Object	15	19%	63	81%	78	100%

3.2 Semantic role and constituent order

This section examines various ways of identifying AGENT and PATIENT in a clause. Cruse (1973) states that there are two main characterizations of agency, those which define it in terms of the surface lexical item "do" and those which define it in terms of extralinguistic facts. For example, Fillmore defines agentive as "the case of the typically animate perceived instigator of the action identified by the verb" (1968:24). Cruse argues, with examples, that Fillmore's agentive case is inadequate because it does not allow for inanimate agents although it hints at allowing them, and because it is difficult on some occasions to decide who is the instigator of the action. Gruber offers a definition similar to Fillmore's but adds the idea of the willfulness of the agent. He defines an agentive verb as one "whose subject refers to an animate object which is thought of as the willful source or agent of the activity described in the sentence" (1967:943). This does not allow for agents that accidentally do something. Cruse comments that these two definitions are inadequate because they attempt to deal with the concept of agent by appealing to extralinguistic facts.

Lyons (1968) mentions the relationship between "doing" and agentivity but does not formulate a test for agentivity. Gruber also notes this relationship and says that an agentive verb is mutually substitutable with the phrase "do something," can be modified by manner adverbials, and can be modified by a purpose clause beginning with "in order to." Cruse contends that, although the "do-test...gives the correct answer in the most obvious cases...[it is] perhaps not as useful as it at first appears" (1973:15).

Cruse (1973), therefore, proposes four features of agency. The first of these is VOLITIVE which indicates an act of the will and can be verified with Gruber's (1967) "in order to" test. The second feature is EFFECTIVE which is something that exerts a force due to its position or motion, not due to internal energy, and allows inanimates to function as agents while contrasting them with instruments. The third feature is INITIATIVE (the term is borrowed from Halliday 1967) and covers those cases where action is initiated by giving a command. This can be tested by the abnormalities which result when (1) the agentivity of the object of the verb is denied, (2) the means of communication between the subject and object is denied, or (3) the responsiveness of the object to the command is denied. The fourth feature is AGENTIVE which indicates that the agent is using its own source of energy to carry out the action. Manner adverbials referring to the energy output of the action can distinguish between agentive and effective agents.

DeLancey (1984, 1985) has discussed the relationship between agency and causation as well as the relationship between agency and syntax. He is particularly interested in agency as it is used in stative/active languages. He suggests that volitional acts express maximal causation, which he illustrates with a causal vector as in (18). As long as two of the items in the vector are present, stative/active languages indicate that the subject is an agent.

(18)   decision to do X   action X   results

A Typological Perspective

DeLancey's causal vector refers to volitional acts. His "decision to do X" is similar to an act of the will which is Cruse's volitive. "Action X" is a volitional act and reflects what Cruse's agentive is able to do by using its own energy source to carry out the action. Cruse's four features of agent cover more possibilities than DeLancey's vector, such as effective which allows for inanimate agents. However, he does not refer to results, as does DeLancey, in any of his features.

PATIENT has been defined in both broad terms and narrow terms. Givón defines patient of state as "the [argument] most likely to appear as subject of state prepositions" and patient of change as "that argument which undergoes the change of state either as the subject of an intransitive or the object of a transitive clause" (1984:88). The traditional definition of patient is the affected recipient of the action described in the verb.

Because Cruse (1973) accounts for the greatest variety of agents, the operational definition here is drawn from his agency features. The operational definition of patient follows the traditional definition presented in the preceding paragraph.

Operational definitions

> AGENT: A NP which exhibits at least one of Cruse's delimiting set of features, i.e., volitive, effective, initiative, and agentive.

> PATIENT: A NP which is the affected recipient of the action of the verb.

DeLancey's vector (1984, 1985) is useful in analyzing the verbs in the clauses. This in turn helps determine which of Cruse's features, if any, the NP exhibits.

The study of semantic roles in relation to Cheyenne major constituent order displays results similar to those obtained in the syntactic research. The agents are divided nearly evenly between preverbal and postverbal positions. The patients follow the verb in 77% of the clauses and precede the verb in 23% of them. Thus, semantic role does not determine constituent order. The tables in (19) and (20) list the numerical results of the counts.

(19) Agent and verb order

	AgV		VAg		Total	
Agent	9	43%	12	57%	21	100%

(20) Patient and verb order

	PtV		VPt		Total	
Patient	14	23%	47	77%	61	100%

Although the overall counts show 118 subject NPs compared to 78 object NPs, notice that there are 61 patient NPs and only 21 agent NPs. As Goddard (1990) explains, the small number of agents compared to the total number of subjects occurs because the agents are more frequently thematic participants who take less overt markings and hence are most often referenced only on the verb.

3.3 Animacy and constituent order

Animate entities are those things which are alive and capable of independent or dynamic activity whereas inanimate entities are not alive and not capable of independent activity. Languages vary as to where and how their grammars make specific distinctions on the animacy hierarchy presented by Tomlin and shown in (21). However, they usually make the splits in such a way that contiguous points on the hierarchy are grouped together.

(21) Tomlin's Animacy Hierarchy (1986:104)

human > other animate > inanimate

MORE ANIMATE ⟶ LESS ANIMATE

The classification of Cheyenne nouns as animate or inanimate basically follows the biological distinction between living and nonliving, but there are exceptions, e.g., 'sun', 'moon', 'star', 'rock', 'ball', some body parts, and some articles of clothing or of personal use are grammatically animate. Trees are also animate while bushes and plants are not. Section 2.2 describes how intransitive verbs must cross-reference the animacy of the subject, and transitive verbs cross-reference the animacy of both the subject and the object.

Hale (1973) and Frishberg (1972) have argued that animacy affects constituent order in Navajo, a language whose basic constituent order is SOV. In Navajo, if both NPs in a clause are equally animate, it is possible to invert the order of the subject and object if there is an appropriate change in a prefix on the verb. However, if the object is animate and the subject is inanimate the subject-object inversion is obligatory.

In Cheyenne, the grammatical classification of a noun as animate is indicated in two ways, i.e., both the plural markings on a noun and the pronominal cross-referencing on the verb must match its animacy. Both of these animacy indicators are independent of constituent order and give us the operational definition.

Operational definition

ANIMATE: A NP classified as animate by Cheyenne grammar

Animate nouns are nearly equally divided in their placement preverbally or postverbally. Thus, animacy is not a contributing factor to the variation in constituent order in Cheyenne narratives. The specific results from the Cheyenne corpus are listed in (22).

(22) Animate noun and verb order

	AnV		VAn		Total	
Animate	51	44%	63	56%	114	100%

3.4 First mention and constituent order

Another parameter which influences constituent order in some languages is the introduction of participants or information needed to understand the narrative. The categories of "new" versus "given" information have frequently been discussed in the linguistic literature. The term "given" is used by Kuno (1972, 1978), Halliday (1967), and Halliday and Hasan (1976) in the sense of PREDICTABILITY or RECOVERABILITY, i.e., the speaker assumes that the hearer could predict that a particular linguistic item would be used in a particular place in an utterance. Chafe (1974, 1976) and Prince use "given" to indicate SALIENCY. Prince says, "The speaker assumes that the hearer has or could appropriately have some particular thing...in his/her consciousness at the time of hearing the utterance" (1978:268). Another use of the term is SHARED KNOWLEDGE as described by Haviland and Clark (1974) as well as by Kuno (1972, 1978). In this use, the speaker assumes that the hearer can access information about a particular thing whether or not (s)he is thinking about it.

Prince (1979) does not use the term "shared knowledge" because it implies a reciprocal relationship between hearer and speaker knowledge, a relationship which may not exist. She prefers to call this kind of knowledge ASSUMED FAMILIARITY and considers it a prerequisite for the understanding of the other two senses of givenness mentioned above. She then goes on to show that there are four kinds of assumed familiarity and three kinds of new information as presented schematically in (23).

(23) Prince's given/new diagram (1979:271)

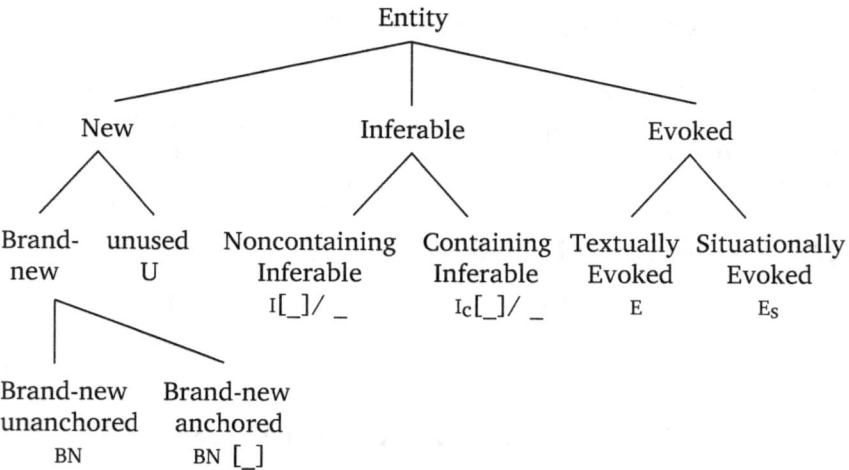

Using an information processing metaphor, one could characterize "Brand-new" as creating a new file. If Brand-new is anchored, it is linked with some other entity, but if it is unanchored, there is no link to any other entity. With unused information, the speaker wants the hearer to reactivate a file. When the speaker assumes that the hearer can identify the reference of an entity through reasoning based on logic or plausibility from what has already been evoked or inferred, the information is called inferable and is like information read in from another file. If the entity has been previously mentioned in the text (textually evoked) or is present in the situation (situationally evoked) then the information is called evoked and is like an open file.

A Typological Perspective

Chafe proposes a cognitive model of information storage and retrieval. He suggests that humans, whether speaker or hearer, have three levels of awareness of information: active, semi-active, and inactive. An "Active Concept ('Given Information')" is one which is currently in focus in a person's consciousness. A "Semi-Active Concept ('Accessible Information')" is something the person is aware of but not concentrating on, something peripheral. An "Inactive Concept ('New Information')" would be one which is in the person's long-term memory but is neither peripheral nor actively in focus (1987:26-31). The speaker re-sorts concepts during pauses while the hearer re-sorts as the information comes in.

Distinct from the given/new classification of information is the identifiability or nonidentifiability of material. Something which has already been referenced in the story would be identifiable, as would be proper names. Christopherson (1939) also presents the idea that information that is evoked by a context can be assumed to be in the hearer's consciousness and thus identifiable. The world and culture of the speaker/hearer would influence the identifiability or nonidentifiability of information and, as Fillmore (1977) proposes, provide information necessary to the full understanding of what is being communicated in the text.

Although not the same as either new or nonidentifiable, first mention of a NP is a nonsubjective way of classifying NPs. However, Chafe and Prince, both of whom discuss the importance of the hearer's consciousness of an item, contend that first mention is not an adequate measure of 'new' nor of 'indefinite'. Payne (1987) also questions the validity of first mention as a means of addressing the identifiability of NPs in a text for two reasons. One is that a number of noninitial mentions in Pima-Papago precede the verb, where her hypothesis predicts new information will be. These follow a lapse of fifteen or more clauses and behave like new information. Thus, it would seem that Chafe's (1976) category of assumed to be or not to be in the hearer's consciousness is more significant than first mention. Secondly, sometimes an item can be inferred from the context, even though it has not been mentioned before. Payne illustrates this with the first mention of "door" following the verb, as Pima-Papago old information does, after a house has been introduced in the text preverbally.

Because first mention is nonsubjectively measurable, it is used in this study as a means of classifying information in the texts. In considering Payne's first reason for disallowing the validity of first mention, Cheyenne also has nonfirst mentions that precede the verb. Out of 128 nonfirst mentions in the texts used, there are 50 which precede the verb. Of these 50, 3 have a lapse of 48 or more clauses between last mention and present mention and 1 has a lapse of 16 clauses; these could, therefore, be considered as reintroductions. They are the only instances where the preverbal noun is acting as new information when it is not the first mention of that noun in the story. In those four cases, first mention is indeed a faulty category, but since these are such a small percentage of the total occurrences and could be considered as new (reintroduced) information, first mention is still a valid means of addressing the identifiability of NPs.

To address Payne's second reason for finding first mention a faulty measure, I subdivided first mention into two groups, those which are nonidentifiable and those which are identifiable from the context. Names, sun, moon, east, father, and similar items are thus classed as identifiable.

First mention and nonfirst mention of information are operationally defined as follows.

Operational definitions

> FIRST MENTION: An expression which has not been previously mentioned in the text. A first mention is further classified as either (a) nonidentifiable, or (b) identifiable if it is a name or can be identified from the context.
>
> NONFIRST MENTION: An expression which has been previously referenced in the text.

In the Howlingcrane texts, first mention NPs follow the verb 71% of the time, nonidentifiable first mention NPs follow the verb 67% of the time, and identifiable first mention NPs follow the verb 77% of the time. In total, first mention occurs before the verb one-third to one-fourth of the time. In (24), the nonidentifiable first mentions are in the first row, the identifiable first mentions in the second row, and the total first mentions are in the third row.

(24) First mention and verb order

	FMV		VFM		Total	
NI	13	33%	26	67%	39	100%
ID	7	23%	23	77%	30	100%
Total FM	20	29%	49	71%	69	100%

A Typological Perspective

The table in (25) demonstrates that for those nouns which reference nonfirst mention information (i.e., people and things previously mentioned in the text), 39% precede the verb and 61% follow the verb. Thus, classifying NPs as first mention or nonfirst mention does not define the order of major constituents in Cheyenne.

(25) Nonfirst mention and verb order

	NFMV		VNFM		Total	
NFM	50	39%	78	61%	128	100%

Mithun (1987) claims that for Cayuga, Ngandi, and Coos, definites tend to come later in the clause than indefinites, even though this is the opposite of Chinese and Indo-European languages including Russian and Czech. To test this possibility for Cheyenne, a NP is defined as definite if it is either an identifiable first mention or a nonfirst mention.

The table in (26) shows that definite and indefinite subjects follow the pattern of subjects as a whole with a nearly random distribution. Definite objects follow the verb almost 80% of the time as do objects as a whole. Although indefinite objects so frequently follow the verb, they only constitute 6% of the sample NPs. Thus, classifying NPs as definite or indefinite does not give insight into the order of the major constituents in Cheyenne narrative.

(26) Definite, indefinite, and verb order

	S/OV		VS/O		Total	
Definite						
SV	43	47%	—			
OV	14	21%	—			
VS	—		48	53%		
VO	—		53	78%		
Subtotal	57	36%	101	64%	158	100%
Indefinite						
SV	12	44%	—			
OV	1	8%	—			
VS	—		15	56%		
VO	—		11	92%		
Subtotal	13	31%	26	69%	39	100%

Cheyenne definites are also marked by demonstratives, either with or without a noun. The demonstrative may be contrastive such as "pitting one established participant against another" (Leman 1985:12), or contrasting one participant with another. The word *tsé'tóhe* 'this one' is often used in such contexts. For example, in a story about a ground squirrel and a turtle who are captured by hunters, the ground squirrel escapes by dancing for his captors and then jumping into his burrow. The captors want to make sure the turtle also does not escape, so they grab him. The turtle starts crawling towards a fire there, so the captors say *tsé'tóhe* 'this one' (the turtle in contrast to the squirrel) *móxhéståhehéhe* 'he must be from there' (the fire).

Most of the examples involving demonstratives in this study are at a point in a narrative where the topic shifts from one participant to another. The table in (27) shows that contrastive or topic shift demonstratives more often precede the verb while other demonstratives pattern the same as definites do, i.e., they tend to follow the verb.

(27)   Demonstrative and verb order

Contrastive or topic shift		Other demonstratives	
DemV	VDem	DemV	VDem
13 72%	5 28%	2 29%	5 71%

Therefore, definite versus indefinite and first mention versus nonfirst mention are not factors in determining Cheyenne major constituent order.

3.5 Tomlin's Theme First Principle

Tomlin (1986) presents three parameters which may affect the order of major constituents in a clause. The first of these is the Theme First Principle (TFP), the second is the Animated First Principle (AFP), and the third is the Verb Object Bonding Principle (VOB). The Verb Object Bonding Principle does not lay any claim to relative order of two NPs, and since in Cheyenne a major constituent can separate an object from its verb, this principle would not provide insight into the order of major constituents in Cheyenne narrative.

One of the early scholars who looked at theme was Mathesius (1939, 1942) of the Prague School. His work was an important source of theoretical ideas, especially regarding theme, for many later scholars. Jones

(1977) summarizes the work of seven European scholars who built on Mathesius and states that "[they] seem to think of theme as a 'point of departure' for an utterance" (1977:53) even though they differ most on how they define that point of departure. The point of departure may be physical (e.g., the first part of the sentence) or psychological (e.g., the beginning/basic idea to which others are connected). The work of these Prague School theorists demonstrates that sentences not only have grammatical components and semantic roles but also carry information about thematic choices. Sometimes the choice of grammatical construction highlights the theme, e.g., a passive construction can identify the patient (goal) as the theme.

Jones (1977:90) charts these seven scholars' differing definitions of theme, their views on the relationship to known or given information, and the levels on which they analyze theme. Jones's table is in (28).

Several scholars use a question technique to identify the thematic elements of a sentence. Consider the following sentence: "The men built the HOUSE," where capitalization indicates the word which carries the most prominent sentential stress. This sentence answers the question "What did the men build?" On the other hand, the question "Who built the house?" is answered by "THE MEN built the house" which, because of a different placement of the most prominent sentential stress, is not identical to the original sentence. Thus, any given sentence answers a particular question. For some scholars, the portion of the sentence which answers the question is the RHEME (the element which carries the greatest degree of communicative dynamism (CD)) and the remainder of the sentence CONTAINS the THEME. Others argue that the answer to a question is the comment portion of the sentence and the remainder of the sentence is the TOPIC or theme.

In her own work, Jones proposes that theme is not just a sentence level phenomenon, but instead other units, such as paragraphs or texts, can exhibit a particular theme as well. She describes theme as "the 'main idea' of a text, a 'minimum generalization' for a text or the 'strucure-defining' backbone of a text" (1977:53). She then defines theme as referential prominence where reference is one of three levels of language, the other two being grammatical and phonological. She says that "reference focuses on the relation of linguistic units to what they are trying to say about 'the world out there' " (1977:5). Following Pike and Pike (1982), she presents four levels of a narrative referential hierarchy, namely identity, event, story, and performative interaction. Since her work deals with expository material, she argues for a four level expository referential hierarchy of concept, point, script, and performative interaction where, for example, an informal proof script would consist of

(28) Theme compared by definition, relationship to known information, and levels analyzed (Jones 1977:90)

	Daneš	Firbas	Dahl	Sgall, Hajičová, Benešová	Halliday
Definition of theme (topic)	Element(s) of lowest CD? or Initial element(s) in sentence?	Element(s) of lowest CD	Left side of logical implication	Contextually bound element(s)	Initial element(s) in sentence
Theme (topic) and known info:	Theme ≠ known info	Theme ≠ known info	Topic = given info	Topic closely associated with given info	Theme ≠ known info; Theme ≠ given info
Levels of themes analyzed	Sentence and text themes (thematic progressions)	Sentence themes only	Sentence themes only	Sentence themes only	Sentence themes only

three points: theorem, arguments, and presuppositions. She proposes that "the *theme of a referential configuration is the nuclear constituent(s) of that unit*" (1977:130) where the term configuration indicates referential units with complex structure. This gives a definition of theme which can be used for any level of language, whether it be sentence, paragraph, section, text, or some other unit. Her studies concentrate on expository English texts, but she suggests that the theme of narrative texts would be the main event line of those texts.

Givón proposes that "thematic continuity is the overall matrix for all other continuities in the discourse" (1983:8), and although it may be the hardest to specify, it is definitely present. He proposes an implicational hierarchy of theme > action > topics/participant. He then describes two operational measures relating to a topic/referent which are (1) referential distance (the number of clauses from the referent/topic to its last previous mention) and (2) persistence (the number of clauses in which the referent/topic continues uninterrupted as a semantic argument of the clause). But, as Tomlin (1986) points out, this measure is linear and not sensitive to the hierarchical organization of discourse. Instead, Tomlin offers a method of measuring a referent's thematic status by computing its CUMULATIVE REFERENTIAL DENSITY (CRD). The computation is outlined in (29).[7]

(29) Tomlin's computation of cumulative referential density (1986:43)

1. Divide the text into paragraphs.
2. Divide each paragraph of the text into clauses.
3. Identify each referent in each clause.
4. Compute the referential density (RD) for each referent in each paragraph using this formula:
   $$RD = \frac{\text{total cumulative references}}{\text{total cumulative clauses}}$$
5. Rank the referents according to their RD score.

This procedure is used to determine thematic information in Cheyenne narratives.

---

[7]See Tomlin (1986:43–44) for an example of the computation of cumulative referential density in English. Appendix A in this book demonstrates the computation of cumulative referential density in Cheyenne.

Operational definition

> THEMATIC RANK: The degree of cumulative referential density at a given point in a paragraph.

The referent with the highest CRD is most thematic at a given point in a paragraph. Other referents at that point in the paragraph are ranked correspondingly.

Since the Howlingcrane texts were transcribed without any discourse segmentation, it was necessary to divide the texts into paragraphs in order to calculate the CRD of the various participants in the texts. A number of linguists discuss paragraphing issues. Tomlin notes:

> The primary drawback to the episode/paragraph approach lies in the difficulty of providing explicit and structure-independent means of identifying episodes and episode boundaries. In this study episodes are argued to be a function of attention allocation, and episode boundaries are identified and manipulated independently of text structure and without dependence on introspection. It may even suggest that in the end discourse units, like the paragraph, are more likely to be the artifacts of linguistic analysis than they are cognitive units utilized by speakers in discourse production. (1987:475)

Other linguists argue that paragraphs ARE a part of discourse. Hinds says, "The basic position that I will advance here is that discourses of all types are organized in terms of paragraphs, a paragraph being defined as a unit of speech or writing that maintains a uniform orientation" (1979:136). Hinds proposes that paragraphs are internally structured in a limited number of segments with certain relationships to the topic of the paragraph.

Both Beekman and Callow (1974) and Longacre argue that a single theme identifies a paragraph:

> We do not simply allege thematic unity; rather, we find it reflected in the surface structure features of the paragraph itself. In narrative discourse, a narrative paragraph is built around a thematic participant, occasionally a small set of thematic participants. In other types of discourse we find the paragraph built around a theme that is not different in kind from a thematic participant. (Longacre 1979:118)

A Typological Perspective

If it is assumed that paragraphs exist, then it is necessary to have some criteria for dividing a text into such units. Grimes (1975) discusses various features that can partition discourses. The first of these is SETTING. A change of scene is usually overtly marked, often near the beginning of the stretch of discourse that has a unified setting. The second is TEMPORAL. Time is always passing, but as long as there is no discontinuity in the time line, the partition can be based on temporal unity. The third feature is SPATIAL. Grimes likens this to different scenes in a play and considers a text section to be a unit unless there is discontinuity in spatial orientation. The final feature is THEME. As long as the speaker maintains the same theme, it can be used as a basis for partition, while a change of theme indicates a new partition. Uniformity in the cast of characters can also be a basis for partitioning discourse, where the cast is viewed as a whole even though some members may be lost or changed (as in a crew on a ship). Grimes' partitioning is thus based on continuity of at least one of these four features.

Larsen (1991a) asserts that even though paragraphing may be a first step in analyzing a text, clear grammatical signals of paragraph boundaries are seldom available. He discusses back reference, full NPs which are not needed to clarify reference, rhetorical questions, and vocatives as possible indications of paragraph boundaries in narrative, although they are not conclusive indicators.

In Philippine languages, Longacre (1970) finds that a characteristic of the nucleus of a narrative paragraph is chaining, where each succeeding sentence recapitulates or explicitly refers to the previous sentence. He goes on to say that paragraphs also have material at the beginning and end which serve to link the paragraph to the surrounding material but "which do not share in the regular sentence to sentence linkage" (1970:55). Sometimes the linkage is in the form of continuance where the verb in the first sentence is continued and completed in the action of the second verb as in Longacre's example of the pair "go" and "arrive." Another example he gives is from the Philippine language Itneg, with the English translation "He *went*" followed immediately by "*when he arrived in the forest*" (1970:65). Chaining as such has not been found in the Cheyenne texts, although there are cases where there are pairs of verbs used in succeeding sentences, such as "leave" and "arrive," which may mark paragraph boundaries.

Longacre argues that the end of a paragraph also serves a special function:

> Whereas in narrative discourse the setting is often used to set the time or the place of a new paragraph, the terminus is often used to take one main participant off the stage or to indicate a lapse of time. The terminus often contains verbs of motion such as *he went away* or *he went off and slept* or *he waited until the next day* or something on that order. (1979:118)

Lord briefly describes narrative paragraphs: "In general, we expect narratives to follow a time sequence; that is, a story typically says, 'Once upon a time X happened and then Y happened and then Z happened and then they lived happily ever after'. Another sequence—that determined by space—is frequently important in narrative..." (1964:30). He also mentions emotional sequence.

Another problem in determining paragraph boundaries concerns quotations. Cheyenne seldom uses indirect quotes but frequently uses direct quotations. Some of the linguistic discussions dealing with theme ignore the quotations. But in several of the Cheyenne texts, the narrative would not hang together without the quoted material.

Longacre's (1970, 1979) insightful treatment of direct quotes is applicable to the Cheyenne texts. He claims that "the orthographic rule in English composition that we must indent for each change of speaker in a dialogue obscures the unity of dialogue paragraphs (where, e.g., assuredly a question and its answer constitute a unit)" (1979:116). He describes dialogue paragraphs as follows:

> Every dialogue involves some sort of exchange. The first speaker solicits the second speaker for information, calls on him to perform some action, or submits some statement for his evaluation. In the first case the first speaker employs some sort of question (not merely rhetorical question but a real request for information). In the second case the first speaker issues some sort of advice, suggestion, invitation, plan, plea, request, or command. In the third case the first speaker simply makes some sort of remark....The solicited replies are respectively: ANSWER, RESPONSE, or EVALUATION. (1970:161)

Longacre also contrasts the use of dialogue in narrative and dialogue paragraphs when he says, "In DIALOGUE PARAGRAPHS *what* one speaker says evokes what the following speaker says with focus on the dynamics of interchange while in NARRATIVE PARAGRAPHS speech EVENTS are simply part of the chain of EVENTS" (1970:68).

A Typological Perspective

Based on the concept of dialogue paragraphs and the place of speech as an event in a narrative paragraph, the definition of paragraph for this study includes dialogue. For purposes of cumulative referential density, dialogue paragraphs are treated in the same way as other paragraphs. The sentences in quotations are counted as regular sentences as are the quote margins, e.g., "he said."

Most of the linguists referred to above agree that a paragraph is a unit of speech or writing that maintains a uniform orientation. The concept of a uniform orientation is the basis for the operational definition of PARAGRAPH.

Operational definition

> PARAGRAPH: A unit of speech which is between two points of discontinuity in spatial, temporal, thematic, participant, or dialogue orientation.

As previously stated, since the definition of thematic rank requires paragraphs within which cumulative referential density (CRD) is computed, it was first necessary to paragraph the Howlingcrane texts, which I did. Another Cheyenne linguist, Wayne Leman, also marked paragraph boundaries in the texts, and he used the English orthographic convention that a quotation marks a new paragraph. There were some places where his choices of paragraph boundaries coincided with mine and others where they did not. Because of the differences, the CRD was calculated both for my paragraph breaks (EP) and Wayne's (WP).

Tomlin's Theme First Principle (TFP) states that the most thematic NP will occur first in a clause. There are only five clauses with two NPs in the Howlingcrane texts. When ranked thematically, one upheld the TFP, three violated it, and one had equally thematic participants. Tomlin (1986) states that the TFP would fail if the ordering is random. In this very small sample, the distribution is random and therefore fails to uphold the TFP.

With such a small sample of clauses with two NPs, it seems inappropriate to simply discard the TFP without looking further to see if there could be a relationship between the most thematic NP and its position relative to the verb. Thematic rank based on CRD with Wayne's paragraphing shows that the participants occur preverbally 33% to 45% of the time and postverbally 55% to 67% of the time as shown in (30). Thematic rank based on CRD with my paragraphing, shown in (31), yields almost the same results, i.e., with a higher percentage of the participants occurring postverbally with the exception of the lowest ranked person.

Since the highest ranked participant does not display a NV configuration most of the time, the degree of thematicity of a NP based on its CRD does not help determine the relative order of a NP in relationship to the verb in Cheyenne.

(30) CRD of a NP and verb order (WP)

Rank	NV		VN		Total	
1	38	38%	62	62%	100	100%
2	23	33%	46	67%	69	100%
3	7	45%	14	55%	21	100%
>3	1	33%	2	67%	3	100%

(31) CRD density of a NP and verb order (EP)

Rank	NV		VN		Total	
1	28	37%	48	63%	76	100%
2	19	33%	39	67%	67	100%
3	14	33%	28	67%	42	100%
>3	6	54%	5	46%	11	100%

To further test whether or not thematic rank influences constituent order, three other methods of ranking a participant were used, i.e., a native speaker's intuition, rank within a paragraph, and rank in the text as a whole.

A Cheyenne speaker, designated as DL, ranked the participants in the Howlingcrane stories according to whether they were main, secondary, or tertiary characters, shown in (32).

(32) Ranking of participants and constituent order (DL)

Rank	NV		VN		Total	
1	33	52%	31	48%	64	100%
2	30	38%	48	62%	78	100%
3	8	15%	44	85%	52	100%
4	1	33%	2	67%	3	100%

Next, using paragraph boundaries, the participant with the greatest number of mentions in the paragraph was given the highest thematic rank and the one with the fewest mentions the lowest rank. Thematic rank

A Typological Perspective

using Wayne's paragraph boundaries is shown in (33), using my paragraph boundaries is shown in (34).

(33) Thematic rank in paragraph and constituent order (WP)

Rank	NV		VN		Total	
1	34	40%	48	60%	82	100%
2	26	36%	47	64%	73	100%
3	9	28%	27	72%	36	100%
>3	2	33%	4	67%	6	100%

(34) Thematic rank in paragraph and constituent order (EP)

Rank	NV		VN		Total	
1	27	51%	26	49%	53	100%
2	21	33%	43	66%	64	100%
3	16	29%	39	71%	55	100%
>3	7	28%	18	72%	25	100%

Another measure of rank is the number of references made to an individual or thing in the entire text, whether it was with a NP or only in the affixes of the verbs. The person or thing mentioned the greatest number of times was given the highest thematic rank and the one with the fewest number of references was given the lowest rank as shown in (35).

(35) Ranking by total number of mentions and verb order

Rank	NV		VN		Total	
1	19	59%	13	41%	32	100%
2	13	45%	16	55%	29	100%
3	6	26%	17	74%	23	100%
4	10	53%	9	47%	19	100%
5–12	23	24%	71	76%	94	100%

Using these six sets of ranking results (30–35), the following observations are noted. The highest ranked participant has a nearly random distribution between preverbal and postverbal positions. The second ranked participant follows the verb about 64% of the time and precedes the verb about 36% of the time. The lower ranked participants follow the verb approximately 70% of the time by all methods of ranking.

These results support the earlier conclusion that a participant's rank in the story does not control the linear placement of an overt NP in relation to the verb in a clause.

These results are not surprising since they are similar to those found in Ojibwa, another Algonquian language. Tomlin and Rhodes (1979) demonstrate that in Ojibwa thematic information is consistently ordered last in a clause, and Tomlin (1986) uses Ojibwa as a concrete example of a language which is a logical exception to the TFP.

3.6 Tomlin's Animated First Principle

Another proposal of Tomlin's (1986), which he calls the Animated First Principle (AFP), is that the NP which is most animated, a combination of agency and animacy, will occur before an NP which is less animated. (See §§3.2 and 3.3 for a discussion of agency and animacy). Several linguists have discussed principles similar to AFP. For instance, Hawkinson and Hyman present data from the Shona language of Zimbabwe and argue that "when appropriate situations can be defined, the more animate participant is assigned to the agentive case. This hierarchy [Natural Topic], which is defined according to which cases have greater access to the more animate nouns in a sentence, parallels that hierarchy given with respect to grammatical accessibility to the subject slot in passive sentences" (1974:161). This accessibility hierarchy is shown in (36).

(36) Hawkinson and Hyman's grammatical accessibility hierarchy (1974:159)

1. Agent: subject agent in simple sentences: embedded agent in causative sentences
2. Benefactive (on behalf of)
3. Dative ('to' of [sic] 'intended for')
4. Accusative
5. Instrumental

Silverstein (1976) proposes a hierarchy, ranking by person and animacy where 1 > 2 > 3 > human > animate > inanimate. (Cheyenne reverses the order of the first two elements ranking 2 before 1.) Although Silverstein's hierarchy is not meant to deal with constituent order, it does demonstrate the prototypical perception of person, agency,

A Typological Perspective

and animacy in languages. Ransom (1977) formulates a general principle that more animate NPs precede less animate ones, in order to explain constituent order in Japanese, English, and Navajo. Schwartz (1974) proposes that the three main elements of a transitive clause are agent, predicate, and patient, with agent usually occurring before patient.

Tomlin demonstrates AFP by showing that although animateness and agency are sometimes independent, at other times they are interrelated. Note the examples of inanimate agents in (37) which illustrate the independence of animacy and agency.

(37) **The clorox** whitened my clothes.
      Our new computer finished those calculations in 132 seconds.
      (1986:105)

Since the prototypical agent is animate, however, agency and animacy are not completely independent. Certain tests for agency, including some manner adverbial tests proposed by Gruber (1967), will fail to identify inanimate agents, and ungrammatical sentences will result such as those in (38) from Tomlin (1986:105).

(38) *The clorox carefully whitened my clothes.
      *The clorox whitened my clothes in order to make me happy.

Not all of the features Cruse (1973) identifies as defining agentivity, namely, volitive, effective, initiative, and agentive, are restricted to animates. In particular, inanimates such as the wind, a moving rock, or a falling plate can exhibit effective features and, thus, be considered animated under certain conditions.

Tomlin suggests an animatedness hierarchy of more animated to less animated shown in (39). Obvious extremes are a human agent and an inanimate patient. A range of cases will fall in between these two extremes, including animate patients and inanimate agents.

(39) Tomlin's Animatedness Hierarchy (1986 43)

      human > other animates > inanimate

      agent > benefactive/dative > patient

      more animated > less animated

Operational definition

> MOST ANIMATED: That NP whose animacy and semantic role in relationship to the predicate is highest on the animatedness hierarchy and which exhibits more of the following qualities: volition, initiative, effective, and/or agentive.

Some grammatical structures of Cheyenne support the Animated First Principle. For example, instead of saying *This shoe fits me* or *My head hurts*, a literal translation of the equivalent Cheyenne expressions would be, respectively, *I fit to the shoe* or *I hurt to my head*, where the animate 'I' outranks the inanimate 'head' and 'shoe'. Also, as described in §2.4, in ditransitive clauses the benefactive/dative is syntactically treated as the direct object regardless of the animacy of the patient because the recipient/benefactor is usually human.

In the Howlingcrane texts, there are five clauses with two NPs; three of these follow the AFP and two do not. Example (40) follows the AFP in that the animate 'one' (i.e., person) precedes the inanimate 'firewood'.

(40) Leman 1980:38.4

> na'ěstse é-s-ta-éve-ame-måheénenán-ǒ-hoon-ǒtse   kåhamaxě-stse
> one   3-PST-away-about-along-gather-INAN-PRET-PL   stick-PL
> One was gathering firewood.

Example (41) does not follow the AFP in that the inanimate 'buckets' precedes the animate 'this'.

(41) Leman 1980:57.69

> mó-me'-ée-hé-heškevo'-óht-a
> DUB-would-about-INT-nick-by^mouth-INAN
>
> ne-ma'kaatóhkonéhan-óts-e   tsé'tóhe
> 2PS-bucket-PL-1PL   this^AN
> This one would surely drain our buckets.

Five clauses are not a large body of evidence on which to base a generalization; however, it does appear that animatedness alone cannot account for preverbal or postverbal position in Cheyenne narrative. The table in (42) shows that the AFP does not determine constituent order for the twenty-one occurrences of animated nouns with verbs.

(42) Animated and verb order

	NV		VN		Total	
Animated	8	38%	13	62%	21	100%

3.7 Payne's combinations of factors

Payne (1987) analyzes Pima-Papago constituent order using combinations of factors. She presents a three part hypothesis for Pima-Papago for information ordering relative to the verb.

a. Nonidentifiable (indefinite) information precedes the verb when the hearer is instructed to open a new active discourse file for it, making it available for further deployment.

b. Pragmatically marked information (including all information question words) precedes the verb.

c. Information for which the hearer is not instructed to open a new active discourse file follows the verb. This includes items for which active cognitive files are already available (e.g., identifiable, or definite, information and uniques), and entities for which files are not to be established, including non-referential mentions. (1987:794)

Cheyenne constituent order follows section b of this hypothesis for Pima-Papago, i.e., all information question words or phrases in Cheyenne precede the verb as do the NPs in the five examples of contrast (*this* person/situation, not *that* one) in the texts. Thus, pragmatically marked information precedes the verb.

If section a were true for Cheyenne, those participants who are nonidentifiable first mentions (§3.4) and highly topical (i.e., ranking 1 or 2) should occur preverbally most often. However, only the nonidentifiable first-ranked by total mentions in text begins to approach the claims of section a. At the same time many of the highly topical nonidentifiable first mentions occur postverbally as shown in (43).

If section c were true for Cheyenne, identifiable first mentions (§3.4) should occur postverbally. However, the table in (43) shows that 28% of the identifiable first mentions and 36% of definites occur preverbally, contrary to expectations. Thus, Cheyenne does not follow sections a and c of Payne's hypothesis for Pima-Papago constituent order.

(43) Summary of tables relevant to Payne's hypothesis, sections a and c

	NV		VN	
Wayne's paragraphing				
Nonidentifiable, first ranked	7	28%	18	72%
Nonidentifiable, first/second ranked	8	23%	27	77%
Elena's paragraphing				
Nonidentifiable, first ranked	6	25%	14	75%
Nonidentifiable, first/second ranked	9	25%	27	75%
DL's ranking				
Nonidentifiable, first ranked	5	31%	11	69%
Nonidentifiable, first/second ranked	13	38%	21	62%
Ranking by total mentions in text				
Nonidentifiable, first ranked	6	60%	4	40%
Nonidentifiable, first/second ranked	9	47%	10	53%
Identifiable first mentions	9	28%	23	72%
Definites	59	36%	103	64%

3.8 Other combinations

For each of the data sets presented thus far, transparencies were made and placed one or two at a time on top of another one so that possible effects on constituent order of two or three parameters at a time could be studied. The tables depicting three parameters frequently had small numbers in their samples so there seemed no point in going beyond three parameters. The resulting tables did not provide strong enough patterns to postulate general rules governing Cheyenne major constituent order based on combinations of factors.

4
Newsworthy First

Chapter 3 looks at Cheyenne major constituent order from several typological points of view and concludes that these produce unsatisfactory results for formulating hypotheses, with distribution percentage sets ranging from 50/50% to 25/75%. Having a quarter or more of clauses as exceptions to a primary order is not an adequate basis for hypotheses.

Mithun (1987) states that constituent order in Coos, Cayuga, and Ngandi is based on the pragmatic consideration of "most newsworthy first." An element of a sentence is newsworthy if it points out a significant contrast, introduces or changes a topic, or represents significant new information. In chapter 4 the tests which Mithun applied to Coos, Cayuga, and Ngandi to demonstrate that they use the Newsworthy First Principle are applied to the Howlingcrane texts to show that Cheyenne patterns in a similar way, thus supporting the hypothesis below. Cognitive support for the hypothesis is also provided.

The following definition and hypothesis are used here to test the possibility that NEWSWORTHY FIRST explains major constituent order in Cheyenne narratives.

THEORETICAL DEFINITION: A major constituent is NEWSWORTHY if it is a significant action, person, or thing, is contrastive, unexpected, new, or needs the hearer's attention.

HYPOTHESIS: In Cheyenne the major constituent, whether it is a subject, object, or verb, which is most newsworthy comes first in linear relationship to the other one or two major constituents in the clause.

The expanded definition for newsworthy, which follows, refers to the newness hierarchy presented in §4.2 (46) where new information precedes inferable information which precedes evoked information (i.e., new > inferable > evoked). This definition also refers to topic shift which is when the point of view of a narrative changes from one participant to another.

> EXPANDED DEFINITION: The higher ranked an action, person, or thing is on the newness hierarchy, the more newsworthy it is. A major constituent, whether representing an action, person, or thing, can also be newsworthy if it indicates a topic shift, is resumptive, is contrastive, or occurs near the peak of a story. Question words and answers to content questions are also newsworthy.

4.1 Newsworthy contrasted with other linguistic terms

Even though linguists already use terms such as rheme, focus, pragmatically marked, and prominent for categories which appear similar to the idea of newsworthy, none of these fully account for linear order in Cheyenne. This section examines each of these terms and compares and contrasts them with newsworthy in order to demonstrate the need for this new term.

The Prague School promoted the study of theme and rheme. As presented in chapter 3, THEME has sometimes been equated with topic, sometimes with the element of lowest communicative dynamism, and, at other times, with initial elements in the sentence. Some of the Prague scholars maintained that theme is not equal to known or given information while others closely associated theme with such information.

In contrast, RHEME is the element with the highest degree of communicative dynamism, or the final element in a sentence, and is possibly associated with new information. The concept of newsworthy can also carry a high degree of communicative dynamism. Both may apply to verbs, although rheme is more likely to apply to a noun in a transitive sentence. The transitivity of a clause in Cheyenne has no bearing on the newsworthiness of any constituent in that clause. Some Prague scholars expect rheme to occur later in a sentence while Cheyenne places newsworthy items initially. In Cheyenne, a NP which some from the Prague School would classify as theme could be newsworthy. This is demonstrated in (30) and (31) which show that, when the most thematic participant is mentioned with an overt NP, 37% to 47% of the time that NP precedes other major constituents of the clause. If newsworthy and rheme were different names for the same phenomenon, newsworthy could not apply to a highly thematic participant. So, although they share some characteristics, rheme and newsworthy are not the same.

Dik presents sentences as having the form "Theme, Predication, Tail" with "Topic and Focus" being part of the predication. He goes on to say that "the Topic presents the entity 'about' which the predication predicates something in the given setting...the Focus presents what is relatively the most important or salient information in the given setting" (1980:15–16). Topic tends to be information shared by the speaker and addressee, unless the speaker presents nonshared information as if it were already shared. Focus usually is not shared information unless a portion of the shared information is being singled out or contrasted with other shared information. Topic lets the hearer know "where to effect a change in his pragmatic information....Focus...contains the instruction as to what change to effect" (Dik 1980:212). Newsworthy and focus share the characteristics of referring to "the most important, most salient information in the given setting" (1980:16). Dik presents both topic and focus as nominal entities in the sentence. Newsworthy, however, is not limited to nominal entities since verbs can also be newsworthy. Thus newsworthy includes focus, as Dik defines it, but is not limited to it.

Payne defines pragmatically marked information as "non-neutral, relative to its communicative force" (1987:787). It includes single and double focus contrast, other contrastive constructions or situations, and information questions and their answers. Pima-Papago texts also demonstrate pragmatically marked contrast at points of change in a major topic, where a major topic is defined as the participant "which a text or subtext is about" (Payne 1987:797). Free pronouns in Pima-Papago frequently appear in single and double contrast situations and so are pragmatically marked. Payne further defines pragmatic markedness as "that information which is to some degree counter to what the speaker assumes are the hearer's current expectations or presuppositional knowledge" (1991:8). A pragmatically marked element would be newsworthy, but newsworthy is not limited to pragmatic markedness in that not all newsworthy entities are counter to the hearer's expectations or presuppo- sitions. In example (44) the egg has been the center of attention, i.e., the man who ate it had rolled it into camp and roasted it while his friend did not want to have anything to do with it and tried to persuade the first man not to eat it. The egg is newsworthy here because, shortly after eating it, the man turns into a water monster. The egg is not being used to correct presuppositions nor expectations because the first man has been insistent on eating the egg all along, nor is the egg used contrastively. Yet that egg occurs initially.

(44) (Leman 1980:38.23)

 héne *vovŏtse* *é-s-ta-mése-no-ho*
 the^INAN egg 3-PST-away-eat-INAN-PRET
 He ate that egg.

Several linguists have argued for using the term prominence for a phenomenon similar to newsworthy. Halliday states, "I have used the term prominence as a general name for the phenomenon of linguistic highlighting, whereby some feature of the language of a text stands out in some way" (Callow 1974:50). In her discussion of prominence, Callow (1974) points out that one must consider the domain over which the prominence extends and what devices signal prominence. Callow states that any entity, whether nominal or verbal, may receive prominence. Both Larsen's (1991b) and Callow's use of the word prominence seem very close to my use of newsworthy, although Cheyenne could have other devices, besides newsworthy first, by which to signal different kinds or levels of prominence. In this case prominence would include newsworthy but would have a wider scope.

Prominence is an all-inclusive term which includes newsworthy, rheme, focus, and pragmatic markedness. Newsworthy includes focus, pragmatic markedness, and rheme but does not completely overlap with rheme. The diagram in (45) depicts how these categories are interrelated.

(45) The relationship between newsworthy, prominence, rheme, and pragmatically marked

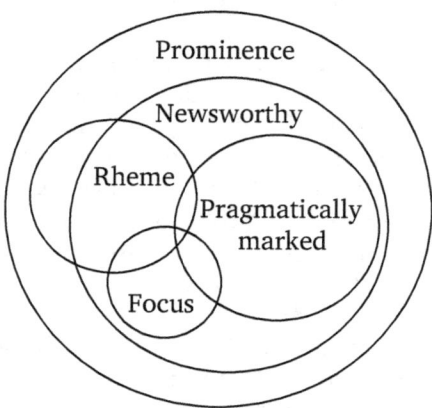

Traditionally, linguists have studied how focus, theme, topic, semantic roles, syntactic roles, and other kinds of information, such as given/new, have influenced constituent order. Often the results of these studies demonstrate how one or another of these factors influences the placement of NPs preverbally or postverbally. When I was considering the study of constituent order solely as the study of preverbal versus postverbal positions, the results of my research were inconclusive. When I stopped considering verbs as the pivot of constituent order, however, and began viewing nouns and verbs on an equal plane, both vying for the clause-initial position as suggested by Mithun's (1987) newsworthy first principle, my research showed promising results.

4.2 Tests for Mithun's newsworthy first principle

Mithun refers to Cayuga, Ngandi, and Coos to demonstrate that contrast is one aspect of newsworthy. She states that "any constituent representing a focus of contrast is generally considered sufficiently important to occur early in the clause, whether it is indefinite or definite, new or old, a topic or not" (1987:302). In the Howlingcrane texts, there are six examples of contrast involving NPs all of which occur clause initially. Contrast is also exhibited by a verb which occurs initially even though the NP following it is brand new and the participant is the highest ranked topic.

Significant new information constitutes another part of newsworthy. Mithun explored old versus new information in the three languages she studied and found that "new information before old information predicts the order of constituents in a large majority of clauses" (1987:296). In cases where constituents are equally new or equally given, "the constituent conveying the principal information of the utterance appears first" (1987:297). She goes on to say that "since new information is usually more important than old information, the principle of new before old usually accounts for constituent order" (1987:287). Mithun gives examples to illustrate "principal information" and "more important" but does not further define these terms.

In the Howlingcrane texts, first mention, whether identifiable or nonidentifiable, follows the verb 67% to 77% of the time (see (24)) if only NPs in relation to the verb are considered. In the five clauses where there are two NPs, three exhibit new before old order and two do not. In those two cases, however, there is a change of participant from the previous clause. Thus, the "newness" of the NPs does not necessarily trigger sentence-initial constituent placement. However, Mithun's work does not limit newsworthiness to nouns, but rather holds that the element which is most newsworthy, whether it is a noun or a verb, occurs clause initially.

In light of Mithun's observations that new information usually precedes old, a newness hierarchy (46) was developed to display this ordering. Prince's evoked information (cf. §3.4) would be included in Mithun's old information since evoked information has been mentioned previously in a text or is present in the situation. Inferable information has not specifically been mentioned before in a text, but it can be deduced through reasoning based on logic or plausibility. The newness hierarchy depicts newest first by having new information preceding inferable preceding evoked.

(46) Newness hierarchy

new > inferable > evoked

In this study, each of the major constituents of a clause, whether noun or verb, was then classified in terms of new, inferable, or evoked. Next, the constituents were charted to see if they followed the linear order of new before inferable before evoked. In 50% of the sample, the verb and noun(s) were either all new, all inferable, or all evoked, 33% demonstrated a newest first order, and 17% reversed the order of two categories of the newness hierarchy. The results are displayed in (47).

(47) New, inferable, evoked, and relative order of words

All new, all inferable, all evoked	95	50%
New before inferable before evoked	62	33%
Evoked or inferable before new, or evoked before inferable	32	17%

Of the 32 that break the newest first rule, 21 are at a newsworthy change of topic from one participant to another; 9 are at the story peak or are crucial to the story line and are also newsworthy; and 2 are unexplained, at this point.

In the Howlingcrane texts, often just before or at the peak of the story, the villain and/or the hero is referred to clause initially, sometimes more than once. It is as if the speaker is telling the listener to pay attention to what this participant or thing is going to do. For example, consider the clauses in (48) which are from the story *The Water Monster*

Newsworthy First 43

(Leman 1980:38); clause numbers are from the interlinear text in that volume. This story is about two young men who set out on a warpath and along the way they stopped to eat. One of them went to get wood for a fire while the other one got out their supplies. Of special interest is an egg that the wood-gatherer finds.

(48) 9. tá'tóhe é-h-ne'-évå-ho'e-ohtsé-hoo'o
that^AN 3-PST-toward-back-arrive-go-PRET

tsé-ta-måhanê-stse
CJT-away-gather^wood-3
The one gathering firewood returned.

10. é-'-ame-ańk-ó'-en-á-no-ho
3-PST-along-around-roll-by^hand-INAN-INAN-PRET

ma'xe-vovôtse
big-egg
He was rolling a big egg.

11. é-x-ho'-ó'-en-á-no-ho
3-PST-arrive-roll-by^hand-INAN-INAN-PRET
He came rolling it.

12. é-s-tå-ho'êstánåhne-hoo'o   tsé-s-ta-éše-éxo'åse-tse
3-PST-away-fire^make-PRET   CJT-PST-away-already-burn-OBV

ho'esta
fire
He built up the fire after it was burning.

13. naa máto   tsé-s-ta-éše-énôse'êstovoo'e-tse
and also   CJT-PST-away-already-end^fire-OBV
And also after there were hot coals,

14. é-s-sé'-o'-en-á-no-ho   héne   vovôtse
3-PST-into-roll-by^hand-INAN-INAN-PRET   the^INAN   egg
he rolled the egg in.

15. é-s-tå-honóht-a-no-ho
    3-PST-away-roast^INAN-INAN-INAN-PRET
    He roasted it.

16. naa   tsé'tóhe   é-s-kánome-mésėhé-hoo'o
    and   this^AN   3-PST-although-eat-PRET
    And this one (supply-man) was eating.

17. vená-he-mėsee-stse
    now-INT-eat-IMP
    "Come eat!

18. né-vé'e-évė-hé-estan-a   vovŏtse
    2-PROHIB-about-INT-take-INAN   egg
    Don't take the egg!

19. é-sáa-pėhéve-nóno'é-háne   é-x-het-ae-hoon-o
    3-NEG-good-appear-NEG   3-PST-say-INV-PRET-OBV
    It doesn't look good," he (supply-man) told him (wood-gatherer).

20. hová'åháne   nė-s-ta-oné'-åht-á-no-ne
    no   2-FUT-away-test-taste-INAN-INAN-1PL
    "No! Let's taste it!

    é-tónėšė-hová'e-vóvota-nėse   é-x-he-hoo'o
    3-how-kind-be^egg-ATTR   3-PST-say-PRET
    What kind of egg is it?" he (wood-gatherer) said.

21. eoto   hé-mėsee-stse   é-'-ŏhkė-het-ae-hoon-o
    acquiesce   INT-eat-IMP   3-PST-HABIT-say-INV-PRET-OBV

    hé-vésen-óho
    3PS-friend-OBV
    "Forget it! Come eat!" he (supply-man) told his friend (wood-gatherer).

22. é-s-ta-éšê-hó'ke-éx-åho'h-á-no-ho
    3-PST-away-already-must-finish-by^heat-INAN-INAN-PRET
    He (wood-gatherer) had to finish cooking it.

    é-'-óo'x-á-no-ho   he-stôhkôxe-va
    3-PST-crack-INAN-INAN-PRET 3PS-ax-OBL
    He cracked it with his ax.

23. héne   vovôtse   é-s-ta-mése-no-ho
    the^AN   egg   3-PST-away-eat-INAN-PRET
    He ate the egg.

The story goes on to tell how the wood-gatherer tries to persuade the supply-man to eat the egg. The supply-man refuses, packs up their supplies, and prepares to leave. The wood-gatherer then turns into a water monster.

In clause 23 the egg is given clause-initial status. It is not brand new since it was introduced in clause 10. This is not a topic shift since the egg is mentioned in clause 22 and continues to be mentioned in the following clauses as delicious and desirable to eat. It is not in contrast with anything else nor is it unexpected that he eat the egg (clauses 20 and 22). Instead, this is a story peak. As Longacre (1983) notes, story peaks are sometimes indicated by changes in the usual method of referring to participants. Since the egg is well established in the Cheyenne narrative, its usual position, if it occurs at all, would be postverbal. Here, however, at the story peak, there are life-changing consequences to eating the egg, so it is given clause-initial position.

Other Cheyenne stories demonstrate a similar phenomenon. In the ten Howlingcrane stories, there are 11 story peaks with just verbs and no NPs, 6 others have a NV order, and 2 have a VN order. In half of the clauses with the major constituents classified for their relative newness, the noun(s) and verb were equally new, inferable, or evoked (47). In those cases where the order was NV (49), the noun carried contrast in 5 cases, and 6 others were nonidentifiable first mentions. In the other cases the nouns mentioned first were in other ways important to the story line. For example, in one story, a girl places her blanket outside as she begins to escape an abusive bear. The blanket, marking the beginning of the escape attempt, occurs clause-initially. In another story a warrior sets out on a warpath to find his friend. In the antagonist's teepee he sees tied-up bundles which later turn out to be his friend's bones. Both the tied-up things and the bones occur clause-initially.

The verb occurs initially in 66% of the clauses where the noun(s) and verb are equally new, inferable, or evoked. One of these is a case of contrast carried in the verb which occurs initially. The table in (49) shows relative constituent order if both the NP and the verb are equally new, inferable, or evoked.

(49) Equal value and relative order

	NV	VN
All new, all inferable, all evoked	32 34%	63 66%

Continuing the consideration of the relative newness of all the major constituents in the clause listed in (47), the newest first order holds 33% of the time. In the 17% of the cases which reverse the hierarchy, the exceptions are for newsworthy reasons (except for the two unexplained cases).

Another facet of newsworthy can be a new topic or new point of view, otherwise known as topic shift. There is a nearly random distribution of preverbal and postverbal NPs at points of topic shift. Thus, topic shift alone does not determine constituent order. However, 67% of the 32 instances when the newest first order was violated (c.f., third line of (47)) were at a point of topic shift, demonstrating that topic shift is a kind of newsworthy phenomenon. The table in (50) displays relative order at points of topic shift.

(50) Topic shift and linear order

	NV	VN
Topic shift	35 58%	25 42%

Upon examining the data to see if the persistence of the participant to whom the topic was shifted has an impact on the choice of position of the NP, it was found that the topic-shift NPs before the verb persisted from 0 to 16 clauses (only 1 of these was more than 9), and the topic shift NPs following the verb persisted for 0 to 10 clauses. Thus, persistence does not control on which side of the verb a NP indicating a topic shift should go.

Another of Mithun's arguments is that "a test for the 'most newsworthy first' principle is provided by questions and answers. Presumably in normal conversation, the most important constituent of an answer is that which corresponds to the interrogative word of the question" (1987:304). In Cheyenne, question words come first in the clause. The Howlingcrane texts have questions but no answers involving a free NP. In other texts found in Leman (1987), most answers to questions did not have both a free NP and a verb, although a few did. There were two LOCV questions, where the location was being questioned. In both replies, the location was the first item in the answer. Two questions regarding the object had it as the first item in both the question and the answer. One question, asking about the subject in a SV order, had a VS answer. Answers to Yes-No questions give the yes or the no first.

Mithun says, "The fact that subjects appear near the end of clauses more often than at the beginning in a pragmatically based system indicates that subjects are typically the least newsworthy" (1987:321). In Cheyenne, the distribution of the subject, whether of a transitive sentence or of an intransitive one, is nearly random in linear position in relationship to the verb. Givón notes that "in human language in context, the subject is overwhelmingly definite" (1979:51), finding that for English discourse, the direct object is the most likely place for the introduction of new referential arguments. In Cheyenne, 77% of the subjects in the texts are definite, but the remaining indefinite subjects constitute 69% of the 44 indefinites in the texts. Cheyenne objects in narrative are 82% definite. Only 2 of the 30 indefinite subjects were agents. These 2 indefinite agents constitute 9% of the 21 total agents in the texts. The other 91% (19) of the agents are definites. Thus, in the texts studied, agents are the most definite of the nouns. Since definites are not new, they are less likely to be newsworthy. Consequently, in Cheyenne, agents are the least likely of the nouns to be newsworthy. In her description of Pima-Papago, Payne (1987) states that new participants are most likely to be introduced as the subject of an intransitive verb or the object of a transitive verb. The same is true for Cheyenne.

Halliday (1967) argues that themes usually appear first in a sentence, since they establish a perspective and an orientation. Mithun (1987) discusses this claim for Coos, Ngandi, and Cayuga, the three languages she studied. She points out that, in narratives, speakers of these languages usually establish the topic very early in the discourse in a way that "fills" an entire sentence or intonation unit. Time, location, and other orienting devices also occur early on. This is also true for Cheyenne. Mithun goes on to say:

If new themes appear early, what of the most common themes, those already established and present in the mind of the speaker? Speakers typically establish a topic and stay with it for a certain length of time. In the absence of counterindications, hearers normally expect the topic to remain constant. Since it is expected, a continuing topic need not occupy a prominent position in the clause. Reference to it within the pronominal prefixes on the verb confirms its continuation without unduly distracting the hearer. The hearer is not actually waiting in suspense until the verb appears with its pronominal markers, since a topic shift would be signalled early in the clause. (1987:308)

4.3 Other support for newsworthy first

In summary then, in Cheyenne, question words come first in a clause and the word which corresponds to the interrogative word of the question comes first in the answer regardless of its syntactic or semantic role. Furthermore, demonstratives used in contrast or at points of topic shift often appear clause-initially, as do nouns or verbs used in contrast.

One construction which Mithun does not list and which supports the newsworthy first principle is a quotation. If a quotation and its quote margin are taken as a unit, the quote almost always comes initially, as in (51).

(51) (Leman 1980:30.6, 7)

    6. ná-ohkė̑-ho'soo'e   é-x-hé-hoo'o
       1-HABIT-dance   3-PST-say-PRET
      "I dance," he said.

    7. naa   vená-ho'soo'ė̑-stse   é-x-hest-óhe-hoo'o
       and   do-dance-IMP   3-PST-say-PSV-PRET
      Well, "Dance!" he was told.

There are 6 examples in the Howlingcrane texts in which there is a quote margin or part of the quote margin before the quote. Three of them use a NP identifying the speaker, followed by what was said, followed by a verb of saying. In these three, the speaker has not been

Newsworthy First   49

referred to for 5, 12, or 21 clauses. For example, in (52), Turtle Moccasin's wife has not been mentioned for 12 clauses.

(52) (Leman 1980:59.138)

    nėhe'še   tsé'tóhe   oha   névé-é'éše   nė-stse-vé'-hovánee'e
    then   this^AN[8]   only   four-days   2-FUT-PROHIB-be^gone

    é-x-het-ae-hoon-o
    3-PST-say-INV-PRET-OBV

Then this one (his wife) told him, "Don't be gone more than four days."

The fourth example, in (53), identifies the addressee, who has not been mentioned for 33 clauses.

(53) (Leman 1980:65.42, 43, 44)

    42. nėhe'še   é-s-tsė-het-ó-hoon-o   he-stotseh-o   néhe
        then   3-PST-CATAPH-say-DIR-PRET-OBV   3PS-pet-OBV   the^AN

        no'kéehe-son-o   he-stseešeeon-e   tsé-ohkė-ho'h-o-se
        squirrel-DIM-OBV   3PS-chest-cn   CJT-HABIT-keep-DIR-3

    43. he   hóovehe   é-x-het-ó-hoon-o
        hey   friend   3-PST-say-DIR-PRET-OBV

    44. o'tóséhe   né'evá-voo-m-ė-stse   é-x-het-ó-hoon-o
        diligently   identify-see-AN-1-IMP   3-PST-say-DIR-PRET-OBV

    Then he told his pet, that little squirrel which he kept on his chest, "Hey, friend, try your best to watch over me!"

The fifth example, in (54), is of an embedded quote by the speaker to his family, the first (inferable) mention of the family in the text, and goes on to give the message for the family.

---

[8]Obviation is not marked on deictics.

(54) (Leman 1980:38.31)

    ta-ně-het-ó-ón-o   *ného'ééhe*   naa   *náhko'ééhe*   naa
    away-CATAPH-say-3-DEL^IMP-PL   1PS^father   and   1PS^mother   and

        na-vóohestot-o   *hétsěhéóhe*
        1PS-relative-PL   here

        ma'-ǒhke-ée-aměˊ-sóhpe-ohtse-vǒtse
        when-HABIT-about-along-through-go-3PL

        ǒhke-anǒh-a'hahtsé-voo'ěse   *hová'éhe*   *tsé-méséˊ-stove-tse*
        HABIT-down-throw-IMP   something   CJT-eat-IMPERS-OBV

        nonohpa   *nåˊ-htse-ohke-ée-mese*
        so   1-FUT-HABIT-about-eat^INAN

Tell my father, my mother, and my relatives: whenever they pass through here, they must throw down something for me to eat so that I will eat it.

In the sixth example, in (55), one participant, a bear, is introduced in the second clause (see appendix C (70)) of the story, and a second participant, a coyote, is introduced in the next clause. The following clause tells of their meeting. Then the quote margin tells us that the bear speaks to the coyote, followed by what was said and a verb of saying. In this case there is a change of attention from the coyote and the two of them meeting, to the bear speaking.

(55) (Leman 1980:27.5, 6, 7)

    5.   *náhkohe*   *é-s-ta-tsěˊ-het-ó-hoon-o*   *ó'kǒhomeh-o*
          bear   3-PST-away-CATAPH-say-DIR-PRET-OBV   coyote-OBV

    6.   *no'hé-hněˊ-stse*
          aside-walk-IMP

7. *hé'tóhe*   *na-meo'o é-x-het-ó-hoɔn-o*
    this^INAN   1PS-path 3-PST-say-DIR-PRET-OBV

The bear said to the coyote, "Move aside! This is my path," he (bear) told him (coyote).

Thus, in five out of the six cases, the unusual placement of the quote margin involves the reintroduction of a character or introduction of inferable characters. The sixth one could be seen as turning the hearer's attention back to the bear after the coyote was introduced. These are all newsworthy reasons for a change in expected order.

4.4 Cognitive support for the hypothesis

Based on unrelated studies, Gernsbacher and Hargreaves (1992) present English-based experimental data and cognitive explanations which shed light on mental processes that support the newsworthy first hypothesis. They describe a wide variety of experiments done by a number of people over the previous twenty years which consistently show that "the information that occurs first in a phrase, clause, sentence or passage gains a privileged status in the comprehender's mind" (1992:84). They propose that the initial word or sentence lays the foundation of mental structures onto which further incoming information is mapped. When incoming data is less related or less coherent, a foundation is laid for a new substructure. Gernsbacher and Hargreaves go on to state that, in experimental situations, "comprehenders recall sentences better when cued by initial words because the initial words form the foundations for the sentence-level mental structures" (1992:88). MacWhinney (1977) has found that both speakers and hearers of English use the first element in a sentence to organize or comprehend the sentence as a whole. Gernsbacher and Hargreaves experimentally demonstrate that the ADVANTAGE OF FIRST MENTION is not related to the agency or subjecthood of the noun in question and that "the advantage of first mention is a relatively long-lived characteristic of the representation of a sentence" (1992:102). They suggest that the speaker will utter initially those words which occur to him first, within the constraints of the grammar of the language, while predicting that so-called 'free constituent order' languages illustrate this placement of most accessible first more transparently than other languages. They refer to cross-linguistic text studies which

> demonstrate the discourse factors that favors [sic] first mention; that is important, focused or newsworthy participants are mentioned first....Important, focused or newsworthy items are likely to be more accessible in speakers' mental representations; therefore, they are likely to be mentioned first. Similarly, their discourse status is also likely to make them suitable foundations for comprehenders' mental representation. In the name of parsimony, we suggest that the privilege of primacy observed in language production, like the privilege of primacy observed in language comprehension, derives from general cognitive processes and the demands of sequential ordering. (1992:109)

Gernsbacher and Hargreaves' work gives independent experimental support to my hypothesis that the most newsworthy major constituent occurs first in a clause, since Cheyenne narratives make good use of the advantage of first mention.

In order to determine what are the logical implications of most newsworthy first, whether verb or noun, I charted several narratives listing only the first linear element of the major constituents of each clause. I found that I could follow the story line just from the list of first elements. Even though 75% of the clauses had only a verb, which carried the action of the story, this exercise did indicate that newsworthy nouns were first in linear order often enough that one could still follow the story line.

5
Experimental Approach to Newsworthy First

5.1 Introduction to the experiment

As stated earlier, the Howlingcrane stories, except for one text, are familiar to Cheyennes as part of their folklore. Such familiarity may produce leaps in the story which both Cheyenne speaker and hearer understand but which escape an analyst. This chapter describes how two videotapes were used to avoid the problem of shared knowledge gaps. The second purpose of this procedure was to test the validity of newsworthy first in a controlled but natural setting which provided standardized texts in that each telling narrated the same scenes in the same sequence. Then sentences about the same scene could be grouped in order to compare which major constituents were used and the order in which they occurred regardless of which speaker or telling is in question. The ten different Howlingcrane texts and seven versions of the Mudhen stories (Leman 1980), which I also examined, did not provide sufficiently cohesive data to test the hypothesis. Two "wordless" videos were used to elicit on-line narration by Cheyenne speakers as they watched the action on the tapes.

The first video, produced by Givón (1991), has some speaking which is not intelligible to an English or Cheyenne speaker. This video is about a man who is working his garden and a woman who fixes his meal. The woman attempts to kill a chicken for his lunch but the chicken escapes. This is called the Chicken video. The second video is a short computer-generated video segment produced by Tomlin which has no speaking. It is about a man who throws a ball for a dog to fetch and is called the Fetch video.

5.2 On-line video narration

Although videos and VCRs are common, Cheyennes had never observed on-line video narration. To illustrate the process to three friends, I narrated the Fetch video in English as I watched it. These friends in turn narrated this video to others who would then narrate the Chicken video. The Fetch video was a demonstration and practice video. It was narrated twice by each of three speakers and once by each of three other speakers. The Chicken video was the control video and was narrated three times by each of four speakers.

I asked my three friends to take turns being a listener as other Cheyennes gave the on-line narrations of the Chicken video. A new listener for each telling would avoid the problem of the speaker using a different strategy or skipping some parts after the first telling because the listener had heard the story before.

Later, the four of us went to visit some Cheyenne friends. Two of the original listeners demonstrated the experiment by one of them narrating the Fetch video in Cheyenne while the other listened. Once a Cheyenne was willing to participate in the experiment, (s)he practiced the procedure by narrating the Fetch video. After this practice, the speaker gave three on-line narrations of the Chicken video. During the first telling, the speakers had never seen the video before and had to base their judgment of what was most newsworthy only on what they had already seen as the video progressed. During the second and third on-line telling of the story, the speakers were now acquainted with the whole story, and made choices as to what was most newsworthy at any particular time, potentially telling the story differently from the initial "cold" description.[9] If the second and third tellings by a single speaker were similar but both different from the first telling, I could conclude that "most newsworthy" is the influencing factor because the only difference between the first and the other tellings is the knowledge of what comes next in the video action. If the speakers had not had an opportunity to practice on-line narration, the differences between the first version and the other two

---

[9]The video description, because it consisted of a chronological sequencing of events, was a narrative. However, since the person seeing it for the first time could only describe what they were seeing, they used descriptive clauses. Once the person knew the events and their order, they could tell it as a true narrative. But in either case, it was helpful in the analysis of most newsworthy as a reason for word order choices.

Experimental Approach to Newsworthy First

could be attributed to lack of practice in the procedure rather than to differences in the perception of newsworthiness.

Because the Fetch video was used as a demonstration and practice video, it was not narrated three times by each speaker, although three people did narrate it twice. Once it was narrated without having previously been seen by the speaker. The other narrations occurred after the speaker had viewed the video, and all but two of these speakers had heard it narrated in Cheyenne by someone else. The Chicken video was narrated three times by each speaker.

On a university campus with laboratories in which to work, it is possible to control the environment in which an experiment is conducted. In that setting, one could expect the participants in an experiment to experience the process in a similar way. No two Cheyenne speakers, however, had exactly the same experience, with the following differences noted:

TR: Observed LF narrate the Fetch video, narrated Fetch II (a slightly different version of the Fetch video), then told the Chicken video three times.

AL: Observed GO narrate the Fetch video, narrated the Fetch video, and told the Chicken video once. Then she went to another room while EK narrated the videos. When EK finished, she narrated the Chicken video the other two times.

EK: Came to AL's house as the experiment was in process with AL, observed AL narrate the last part of her first telling of the Chicken video, narrated the Fetch video, and then narrated the Chicken video three times.

IR: Observed me narrate the Fetch video in English before narrating the Fetch video twice and the Chicken video three times. There were no Cheyenne speakers as listeners.

The protocol for this experiment consisted of a demonstration of on-line video narration by a Cheyenne person narrating the Fetch video in Cheyenne or by my narrating the Fetch video in English. Although protocol varied for each speaker, the variations in protocol did not affect the outcome of the experiment, since the purpose of the protocol was to demonstrate how to do the experiment and give the speakers an opportunity to become comfortable with the procedure. The experiment consisted of eliciting the on-line narrations of both videos which was accomplished regardless of the protocol.

The listeners did not take turns sitting in a chair just behind the video. They simply were in the room with the speaker and me. The speakers were so intent on narrating the video that they did not pay any attention to the listeners. The listeners provided moral support to the speaker by telling how they had each done the task, by demonstrating the task, and by being an encouragement while the speaker did the practice run.

Two of the ladies complained about the pace of the videos as they attempted to narrate what they were seeing. They said the videos went too fast to allow them time to think of the best words, even though Cheyenne is their first language, their language of preference, and "has just the right word to describe almost anything." The pace of the videos frustrated them, not their language ability.

Narrating the video three times in succession produced some interesting effects. At least once, at the beginning of the third telling, a speaker referred to the first participant in the first scene as definite even though he was brand new in the video. On the third telling, TR seemed to speak a bit ahead of the video sequence, anticipating what was to come since he knew the story well by then.

I tape-recorded all of the on-line narrations of both videos. Then GO, a Cheyenne friend, and I transcribed the tapes. GO would listen to a section of tape, repeat each word slowly for me while I wrote it, then translated it.

I took the computer printout of the transcribed tapes to AK, another Cheyenne friend. AK listened to the tapes and put punctuation in appropriate places. She then worked from a printout without an English translation to give me a free English translation that was close to the translation GO gave me, with some refinement in the meanings of some of the words. AK also clarified the relationship between noun and verbs in those cases where a noun was between two verbs and I did not know to which verb the noun belonged.

In §3.5, I described the difficulties I faced in marking paragraph boundaries on the Howlingcrane texts. With the videos, even though I once again had a long string of clauses with no paragraphs marked, the episode boundaries are already determined. Hayashi (1990) has done extensive analysis of the Chicken video dividing it into three types of units. One type is that of ENCOUNTERS following Warren, Williams, and Shaw (1985) and defined as follows:

Experimental Approach to Newsworthy First 57

> An encounter is 'an ecological event' in which an animal participates either as an actor or as a perceiver preparatory to action. We define action as intentional behavior. Hence, encounters are events pregnant with information relevant to the control of action. (Hayashi 1990:23)

Hayashi divides the video into encounters between various entities in the video such as woman:matches, woman:log, and woman:match:fireplace. He then lists events under each of the encounters using a second type of analysis called SMALL CHANGE ANALYSIS, frame by frame. The third is NEW OBJECT/PARTICIPANT ANALYSIS in which only encounters with new participants or objects are recorded, where "new" includes those participants or objects which have left the scene but are later accessible.

Although these three types of encounters are too fine to be usable as episode boundaries in the Cheyenne on-line narrations, Hayashi presents another unit which works well. At those segments in the video where the same action continues for quite some time, or where there is no one in the scene, e.g., places where the viewer wonders "what's next?", he predicts and finds clause-final intonation, as opposed to nonfinal intonation contours at those segments where the viewer "is able to anticipate the next event and its connectivity to the previous event" (1990:32). These "what's next?" places provide predetermined episode boundaries in the video texts which avoid circular reasoning in marking paragraphs and provide consistent paragraph breaks in all the texts.

Following is a compilation of the English translation of the various Cheyenne narrations of the Chicken video. Like phrases describing the same scene are grouped into frames.

1. A man is walking.
   He's going to work.
   He's carrying his tools. His tools are used for planting a garden.
   He puts his tools there (by a tree).
   He put them away neatly.
   One fell down.
   He picked it up.
   He took his ax.
   He carried it.
   Sticks are piled up.
   He chops the sticks. / He makes kindling.
   He cuts them in small pieces (for his fire).
   He tosses the sticks. / He keeps cutting.
   He quit. / He has enough. / He stands up.

2. She called him. / He saw her.
She comes to him. / Lady is walking.
They talk.
(S)he tells her (him) about the sticks.
Branches are lying there. / They/sticks are piled up.
Maybe they are for starting a fire.
She's walking. / She keeps carrying (something).
She came to the branches.
She breaks the sticks by hand. / She breaks them (by stepping on them).
She picked them up. / She piled them up.
She is going to start a fire with those sticks.
She carried them. / She left. / She's walking (around).

3. Man quit chopping sticks.
He leaves (without the sticks).
He carries his ax.
He's going.
Some of his tools are right there.
He put down his ax.
He picked up his tools. / He put his tools away. / He carries his tools (over his shoulder).
He walked away. / He walks across bare ground.
Trees are growing there.
He's going towards them.

4. Woman came (around).
A house is there.
She went/came around it.
She passed it.
She carried the sticks.
She's going to make a fire.
She walked to them.
Rocks (animate) are there (piled up). / She piled them up. / She fixes it.
They cook there.

5. Rocks are in a circle.
She put them down (sticks).
She left. / She's walking towards it.
She's walking back.
She picked it up (something). / She picks up matches.

Experimental Approach to Newsworthy First 59

She starts the fire. / She lights/strikes them.
She piled it up.
She adds more sticks and leaves. / She started it with leaves.
She puts them on top.
It starts burning. / Sticks start burning.
She added more sticks.
There are flames. She did a good job.

6. She picked up her pot.
She carries it. / She's walking.
She's walking towards it (big water pail).
Water (pail) is there.
She pours water (into her pot).
She carries it. / She's walking.
She put it on the fire.
She is going to heat it.
She adds more wood.
She puts the wood down.
She brushes off her hands.
She left/walked away.
She went towards the little house.

7. She's walking.
She went around/inside that little house.
She's gone for awhile.
She goes around again. / She comes (back around).
She's carrying something/bird/chicken.
She brings it over.
She brings him/it to where they cook.
She picks up her knife/ax.
She's going to cut off the chicken's neck.
The chicken is really hollering.
She tries to hold him. / She can't hold him good.
She holds him different ways. / She's got him under her arm.
She puts down her knife.
He tries to get away. / The chicken slipped/escaped. / He got away. / That chicken took off.
She chases him.
He got away.
She gives up on him.
Chicken runs for his life.

8. She's walking. / She's coming back.
She's walking towards the little house.
She opened the little house.
She got something out.
It's wrapped (in rags).
She carried it. / She took/put it on her work/cooking place.
She grabs it.
It's wrapped.
She unwrapped/opened it.
She took it out. / She's taking it out (of paper).
She picks up her knife.
She cut it up. / She sliced it (into small pieces).
She's fixing it slowly.
She's done cutting it. / She put it down (on the paper).
She wrapped it up again. / She put it away.
She put her knife down.
She left. / She took it. / She carried it.
She's walking. / She's walking across.
She passed that little house.

9. The man is working/digging/hoeing.
He's hoeing his garden. / He's planting a garden. / He's digging.
She got to where he's working. / The lady got there.
They're talking. / The man talks to the lady. / The lady talks to the man.
He puts his tools down.
He/they sat down.
They sat where it is shady.
They/he are going to eat.
She came to feed him. / She gave him what she fixed.
He looked at it/opened it.
He doesn't want it. / He didn't like it. / He didn't eat it.
He got angry. / He's talking.
He threw it in front of himself. / He threw it at her.
She goes for him. / They argue/fight.
He picks up his hoe.
The man chases the woman. / They chase each other. / They chase around a tree.
He's carrying something. / He's running with something.
She's screaming.
He almost catches her. / He can't catch her.

After I taped the on-line narrations, transcribed, translated, punctuated, and paragraphed the texts, I analyzed the data. The results are presented in the next chapter.

6
Results of the Experiment and Newsworthy First

The on-line video narratives produced a total of 976 clauses of which 799 were from the Chicken video and 177 were from the Fetch video. The percentage of clauses with overt NPs in the video narratives is higher than in the Howlingcrane texts. The Fetch video has an especially high percentage of clauses with an overt NP. The table in (56) displays these percentages.

(56) Comparison of percentages of overt NPs in texts

	Total # of Clauses	Clauses with 1 NP	% of Total	Clauses with 2 NPs	% of Total
Howlingcrane	810	204	25	10	1.0
Chicken	799	264	33	20	2.5
Fetch	177	108	61	6	3.4

Out of a total of 976 clauses in the video narratives, there are only 26 clauses with three major constituents. All but one of the six possible orders of constituents is used. The table in (57) shows the distribution of the three major constituents in these 26 clauses from the video experiment. The table also includes clauses from the Howlingcrane texts and from seven Mudhen stories (taken from Leman 1980) which have three major constituents.

(57) Distribution of clauses with three constituents

	Chicken video	Fetch video	Howlingcrane	Mudhen	Totals
SVO	10	6	3	0	19
VOS	4	0	2	1	7
OVS	3	0	0	0	3
SOV	2	0	0	0	2
OSV	1	0	0	0	1
VSO	0	0	0	2	2

For convenience I repeat the definition of newsworthy and my hypothesis which I presented in chapter 4.

THEORETICAL DEFINITION: A major constituent is NEWSWORTHY if it is a significant action, person, or thing, is contrastive, unexpected, new, or needs the hearer's attention.

HYPOTHESIS: In Cheyenne, the major constituent, whether it is a subject, object, or verb, which is most newsworthy comes first in linear relationship to the other major constituent(s) in the clause.

Recall that the newness hierarchy presented in §4.2 (46) has the order of new > inferable > evoked, and that a topic shift occurs when a narrative moves from the point of view of one participant to another. An expanded definition for newsworthy, then, is as follows.

EXPANDED DEFINITION: The higher ranked an action, person, or thing is on the newness hierarchy, the more newsworthy it is. A major constituent, whether representing an action, person, or thing, can also be newsworthy if it indicates a topic shift, is resumptive, is contrastive, occurs near the peak of a story, is a question word, or is the answer to a content question.

The on-line video narrations support my hypothesis if there is a newsworthy reason for having a constituent come initially in the clause; or if the constituent order is not the same, there is a newsworthy reason to account for the alternate order(s).

Many times the speakers agreed on which participant(s) or item(s) referenced by the verb would be expressed with an overt NP. If they all chose to express the object with a NP, then I listed their choices as VO or OV depending on the relative order the speakers used in the clause. I followed the same practice if the speakers chose to express the subject with a NP. There were times, however, when, in the same frame, (1) some of the speakers chose to use a NP for the subject but not the object, (2) others chose to use a NP for the object but not the subject, (3) some chose to use only a verb, and (4) others used a NP for both the subject and the object. For example, in the Fetch video there is a frame where the dog is walking towards the man. This frame is charted in (58). One speaker used only a verb, line a. Two speakers used a NP for the subject as well as a verb, lines b and c. Another speaker used a verb and an object noun, line d. The last one used two NPs along with the verb, line e.

    I first divided the four clauses which used NPs into two groups, those with VO and those with SV. This gave me the relative order of the dog to the verb and the man to the verb. In this frame, only lines b and c have the same constituents. If I considered only the clauses with the same constituents, I would lose the information that when a NP was used for man, it was in the same relative position in the clause. I would also lose the information that when a NP for dog was used, it also was in the same relative position in the clause. Then, by limiting myself to an OV/VO choice or an SV/VS choice at each frame, I was able to divide each frame into a majority and minority choice for each noun in relationship to a verb. An example frame from the Chicken video is given in (59). In this frame, out of 12 narrations, a majority of 8 chose a VO order for the verb and object while a minority of 2 chose an OV order. There is a majority count of 2 SV orders and no minority count for VS. The two clauses with an S were the first clauses the two speakers used for that telling of the video. The two SVO clauses are also compared with 24 clauses from other frames that also have three major constituents.

(58) Fetch video frame 14

Speaker	Constituent Order			
a. TR	V		é-nêx-ho'ĕhót-áá'e 3-toward-arrive-OBV^INV	O
			He comes to him.	
b. AL	SV	tá'tóhe oeškeso that^AN dog	mó-'-ame-nó'-ôhtsé-'tov-ô-he-vó-he 3-PST-along-approach-go-AN-DIR-NEG-OBV-NEG	O
		The dog goes toward him.		
c. EK	SV	oeškeso dog	é-nó'-ôhtsé-'t-óó'e 3-toward-go-AN-OBV^INV[10]	O
		The dog goes toward him.		
d. IR2	VO		é-s-ta-nôhts-ĕhót-ô-hoon-o 3-PST-away-approach-AN-DIR-PRET-OBV	hetan-óho man-OBV
			He walked towards the man.	
e. IR1	SVO	oeškeso dog	é-s-ta-ame-nôhtsĕhót-ô-hoon-o 3-PST-away-along approach-AN-DIR-PRET-OBV	hetan-óho man-OBV
		The dog walks towards the man.		

---

[10] This clause is sandwiched between two clauses in which 'the man' is proximate. I would have expected 'dog' to be obviated. However, in checking this section with another native speaker, the meaning of the sentence came across clearly as 'the dog goes towards the man'. The second speaker stated that it would probably be best if 'the dog' had been obviated, but it was clear from the context that the 'dog' was walking, not 'the man'.

(59) Majority/minority counts in chicken video frame 3

Speaker		Constituent order	
AL1		V	O
AL2			
AL3	S	V	O
EK1		V	O
EK2		V	O
EK3		V	O
IR1			
IR2	S	V	O
IR3		V	O
TR1		O	V
TR2		O	V
TR3		V	O

The table in (60) displays the number of times the various speakers chose the same order for a verb and its NP and the number of times the various speakers chose a variant (minority) order. It is interesting to observe in (60) that the Fetch video elicited a greater uniformity in word order than did the Chicken video. One could speculate as to the reasons for this: e.g., the Fetch video is shorter, it has fewer items, or its background remains basically constant. Although the choices for order in the Fetch story had a minority order only 12% of the time, the choices in the Chicken video show a variation 24% of the time. The Chicken video results are similar to results obtained using typological methods of investigation of constituent order in chapter 3. Further investigation is needed, however, to discover why in certain cases the speakers used the opposite order from the majority and if there is some newsworthy reason for minority versus majority choice.

(60) Variation from the majority choice for word order

	Majority	Minority	Total	% of variation from majority
Fetch	101	14	115	12
Chicken	236	73	309	24
Total	337	87	424	20

A closer look at the results of the experiment showed that there are newsworthy reasons for the speaker's majority choices. For example, in the sixth episode of the Chicken video, when the woman is about to cut off the chicken's neck, all five speakers who mention the chicken do so clause initially. Three of these instances immediately follow the first mention of the knife, the fourth is the first mention of the chicken, and the fifth is the first identification of the thing being carried as a chicken. Topic shift, first mention, and first identification are all newsworthy reasons to be clause initial. Another example comes from the first episode of the Fetch story, where a man is walking and a fountain comes into view. All four speakers who mention this place the new, newsworthy water clause initially. In the second episode of the Fetch video, the dog jumps over a rock. All nine speakers chose to place the new, newsworthy verb before the new rock. The table in (61) displays the newsworthy cases where all the speakers agreed on the order of the words.

(61) Newsworthy majority choice for word order

Fetch	55
Chicken	65
Total	120

I examined the texts looking at all cases where there was variation in order for a single frame. For example, in the Chicken story, the third episode consists of frames where the man quits chopping wood, carries his ax over to his other tools, picks up his tools, and then walks off. In the third frame, seen in (62), where the man carries his ax, three tellings have an OV order (62 a,e,f) and three a VO order (62 b,c,d). All three VO tellings follow a sentence which translates as 'The man stopped wood-chopping', where the ax is inferable and thus is lower on the newness hierarchy than the verb for carry. Two (62 a,e) of the three tellings which have an OV order are the first clause of this episode and have three major constituents. The man in this third episode represents a topic shift from the woman who is the main actor in the second episode. Topic shift is a newsworthy reason for the man to occur clause-initially. The ax/hatchet in each of the three clauses with OV order is a resumptive first mention which is a newsworthy reason for the ax/hatchet to occur before the verb. Therefore, there are newsworthy reasons for the use of both the VO and OV orders in this particular frame.

(62) Chicken video, third episode, third frame: 'He carries his ax.'
Comments in parentheses give newsworthy reason for order.

    a.   AL second telling

S	O	V
tá'tóhe hetane	he-stóhkȯxe	é-ta-éva-ame-no'e-ohtse
that^AN man	3PS-ax	3-away-back-along-with-go

That man carried his ax.
(topic shift, man: resumptive first mention, ax)

    b.   AL third telling

V	O
é-ta-éva-ame-no'e-ohtse	he-stóhkȯxe
3-away-back-along-with-go	3PS-ax

He carried his ax.
(new verb)

    c.   EK first telling

V	O
é-éva-ase-no'e-ohtse	he-stóhkȯxe
3-back-off-with-go	3PS-ax

He carries off his ax.
(new verb)

    d.   EK third telling

V	O
é-éva-ase-no'e-ohtse	he-stóhkȯxe
3-back-off-with-go	3PS-ax

He carries off his ax.
(new verb)

e. TR first telling

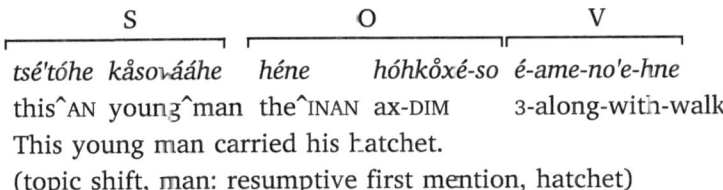

S	O	V
tsé'tóhe kåsovááhe	héne hóhkóxé-so	é-ame-no'e-hne
this^AN young^man	the^INAN ax-DIM	3-along-with-walk

This young man carried his hatchet.
(topic shift, man: resumptive first mention, hatchet)

f. TR third telling

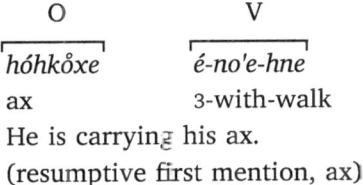

O	V
hóhkóxe	é-no'e-hne
ax	3-with-walk

He is carrying his ax.
(resumptive first mention, ax)

In the frame where the man picks up his tools, eight tellings refer to the tools with an overt NP following the verb, while one telling uses a NP for the tools and places it before the verb. For that one telling, this is the first reference to tools in this episode, and therefore it has initial position. All the other tellings have already mentioned either the tools as such or the ax, which is a specific member of the man's group of tools. Thus, it is newsworthy to mention what he did with the tools in a VO order.

Since the texts resulting from the video experiment exhibit the variation shown in (60), I looked to see if a newsworthy reason accounts both for majority choices and the alternate order, when there is one. First consider the relative order of the verb and one other major constituent, whether it be subject or object. The table in (63) shows that there are newsworthy reasons for agreeing on the order of constituents or there is a newsworthy explanation for the variation in 94.1% of the clauses. These results support my hypothesis.

(63) Newsworthy variation and majority choice for 2 constituents

	Newsworthy majority or newsworthy alternate	Can't explain minority alternation	Total	% with newsworthy order
Fetch	110	5	115	95.7
Chicken	289	20	309	93.5
Total	399	25	424	94.1

Next consider the relative order when there are three major constituents in a clause. The table in (64) shows that there are newsworthy reasons for agreeing on the order of constituents or there is a newsworthy explanation for the variation in all of the clauses. These results also support my hypothesis.

(64) Newsworthy variation and majority choices for three constituent clauses

	Newsworthy majority or newsworthy alternate	Can't explain alternation	Total	% with newsworthy order
Fetch	5	0	5	100
Chicken	13	0	13	100
Total	18	0	18	100

In all the clauses for which I could not find a newsworthy reason for the alternate word order, all the constituents were equally old. For example, in the fifth episode of the Chicken video the woman is busy building a fire. The Cheyenne narratives of one frame could be roughly translated 'She added more sticks' and have two clauses with an OV order (65 a,b) and two with VO (65 c,d). Building the fire, adding sticks, and the fire itself have been on the scene for a while so there is no topic shift. All the participant/actions are expected and all are equally old. If the sticks had not been previously mentioned in the episode, one would expect the OV order. Or if the sticks had been mentioned recently, one would expect a VO order. However, before this frame the sticks were previously mentioned about the same number of times in each of the four tellings. The factors which influence constituent order, topic shift, old versus new, and previous mentions are all equal for the clauses in (65) and yet there are both VO and OV orders.

(65) Chicken video, fifth episode, eleventh frame

    a.   AL second telling

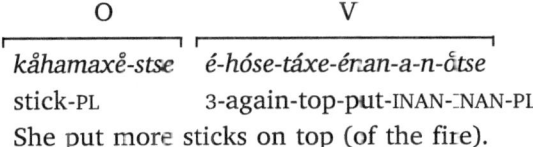

O	V
kåhamaxê-stse	é-hóse-táxe-énan-a-n-ôtse
stick-PL	3-again-top-put-INAN-INAN-PL

She put more sticks on top (of the fire).

    b.   TR first telling

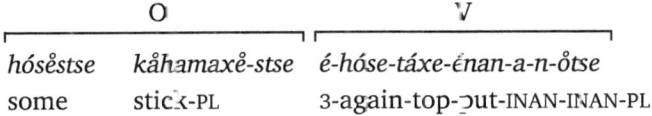

O		V
hósêstse	kåhamaxê-stse	é-hóse-táxe-énan-a-n-ôtse
some	stick-PL	3-again-top-put-INAN-INAN-PL

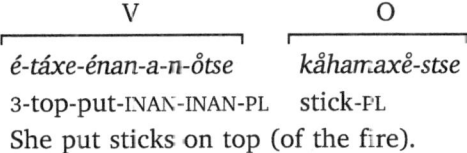

S	
néhe	kåse'éehe
the^AN	young^lady

The young lady put more sticks on top (of the fire).

    c.   AL third telling

V	O
é-táxe-énan-a-n-ôtse	kåhamaxê-stse
3-top-put-INAN-INAN-PL	stick-PL

She put sticks on top (of the fire).

    d.   EK third telling

V	O
é-hóse-táxe-énan-a-n-ôtse	kåhamaxê-stse
3-again-top-put-INAN-INAN-PL	stick-PL

She put more sticks on top (of the fire).

Each speaker narrated the Chicken video three times. I investigated whether there was a pattern where either all the tellings by a single speaker were the same or, when there was variation, if the first telling was different from the other two. Knowing the whole story could affect

Results of the Experiment and Newsworthy First

how the speaker interpreted newsworthiness at particular points in the video, and the second and third tellings could reflect this interpretation. However, I found instances of all four possible variations in constituent order by a single speaker as shown in (66).

(66) Examples of the variations in constituent order by the same speaker narrating the Chicken video. Comments in parentheses give newsworthy reason for order.

    a.   All the tellings have the same constituent order

        EK first, second, and third tellings, second episode

V	O
é-hé-estan-a-n-ôtse	kåhamaxê-stse
3-INT-take-INAN-INAN-PL	stick-PL

She took some sticks.
(new verb)

    b.   First telling different constituent order from other two

        TR first telling, first episode

S	V
kåhamaxê-stse	é-hóne'tan-et-otse
stick-PL	3-be^piled-PL-OBV

Sticks are piled up.
(inferable sticks and pile)

        TR second and third tellings, first episode

V	S
é-hóne'tán-êstse	kåhamaxê-stse
3-be^piled-PL	stick-PL

Sticks are piled up.
(new verb)

c. First and second telling, same constituent order; third telling different

TR first telling, first episode

O	V
hóhkŏxé-so	é-no'e-ohtse
ax-DIM	3-with-go

He's carrying a hatchet.
(new hatchet)

TR second telling, first episode

O		V
héne	he-tsêhetaneon-ôtse	é-no'êst-o'xé-ohtse-n-ôtse
the^INAN	3PS-tool-PL	3-over-on^back-go-INAN-PL

He carried his tools over his shoulder.
(new tools)

TR third telling, first episode

V	O
é-ame-no'êst-o'xé-ohtse-n-ôtse	he-tsêhetaneon-ôtse
3-along-over-on^back-go-INAN-PL	3PS-tool-PL

He's carrying his tools over his shoulder.
(new verb)

d. First and third telling, same constituent order; second telling different

EK Chicken video first and third tellings, third episode

S	V
hetane	é-éne-ó'xoe-måhane
man	3-end-chop-firewood

The man quit wood-chopping.
(resumptive first mention, man)

EK Chicken video second telling, of third episode

V	S
é-éne-ó'xoe-måhane	tsé'tóhe
3-end-chop-firewood	that^AN

That one quit wood-chopping.
(resumptive first mention, verb)

Example (67) displays the variation in tellings in a particular frame by the same speaker when a given speaker uses a NP for the same person/object in all three tellings. It includes the narrations of all the speakers. The results (rows a and b) show 32 instances where either all the tellings by a single speaker are the same, or the first telling is different from the other two. There are 12 exceptions (rows c and d), where, for a single speaker, either the first and second tellings are the same and the third one is different, or the first and third telling are the same and the second one is different.

(67) Variation in constituent order in tellings by same speaker

a.	23	All the tellings are the same
b.	9	First telling different from other two
c.	9	First and second telling same, third different
d.	3	First and third telling same, second different
	44	Total examples with one speaker using a NP in all three tellings

For each of the 12 instances in rows c and d there is a newsworthy reason for the alternate order. In 10 of these, however, it is not clear why the speaker chose the second telling or the third telling to use the alternate order. These results (c and d) do not falsify my hypothesis because there are newsworthy reasons for the alternate orders as well as for the majority orders. Instead, they show that newsworthy is a dynamic process dependent on the choices the speaker makes at the time of speaking.

There was an 87.5% correlation between the first mention of a major actor in a new episode (resumptive mention) and clause initial position, which is expected since major actors are important to the story. This strong correlation accords with my hypothesis of newsworthy first.

Some questions remain about Cheyenne major constituent order. What influences a speaker to use alternate orders at the unexpected places? Is it the same thing which influences choices when all constituents have the same value on a particular parameter, such as when all of them are new, or when all of them are old? Where there are different newsworthy reasons for alternate orders, what influences the choice of one newsworthy reason over the other? How does newsworthy first interact with placement of other words in sentences, such as time words, adverbials, demontratives, and the heads of relative clauses? Does newsworthy first influence the order of discourse level constituents? These questions are left for future study.

7
Conclusion

This book has explored the factors that influence the order of major constituents in Cheyenne narrative. Using ten texts of varying lengths by the same author, I studied whether the following factors influenced the placement of a noun before or after the verb: syntactic role, semantic role, first-mention, nonidentifiability, animacy, thematic rank, a native speaker's ranking of participants, and rank by total number of mentions in the paragraph or text. Nouns followed the verb 50% to 75% of the time with some of the preceding factors having a stronger tendency than others to order the noun after the verb.

I examined Cheyenne to see if it followed Tomlin's (1986) basic constituent order principles. For both the Theme First Principle and the Animated First Principle, I was unable to make a generalization because there were only five clauses in the texts I studied which have two overt NPs with different syntactic roles in the same clause. I further investigated whether thematic rank or animatedness could influence the placement of a noun preverbally or postverbally. The results of both studies were random or of insufficient strength to support an argument that these factors determine constituent order.

I tested Payne's (1987) hypotheses for Pima-Papago to see if they were upheld in Cheyenne. Her hypothesis that pragmatically marked information (including information question words) precedes the verb held for Cheyenne. Her other two hypotheses do not hold for Cheyenne, i.e., indefinite information available for further deployment occurs postverbally, and information for which the hearer is not instructed to open a new file occurs postverbally.

I studied whether combinations of factors controlled constituent order. The results were as inconclusive as were the results of the above mentioned studies of single factors.

Since typological explanations of constituent order could not account for 25% to 50% of the nouns preceding the verb, I investigated Mithun's (1987) claim that in Coos, Cayuga, and Ngandi the most newsworthy item appears clause-initially. Because the newsworthy first principle provides a more complete accounting of Cheyenne constituent order, I adopted it as a model for my research. I defined newsworthy and presented my hypothesis (c.f. chapter 4) which are both repeated here.

THEORETICAL DEFINITION: A major constituent is NEWSWORTHY if it is a significant action, person, or thing, is contrastive, unexpected, new, or needs the hearer's attention.

EXPANDED DEFINITION: The higher ranked an action, person or thing is on the Newness Hierarchy, the more newsworthy it is. A major constituent, whether representing an action, person, or thing, can also be newsworthy if it indicates a topic shift, is resumptive, is contrastive, or occurs near the peak of a story. Question words and answers to content questions are also newsworthy.

HYPOTHESIS: In Cheyenne, the major constituent, whether it is a subject, object, or verb, which is most newsworthy comes first in linear relationship to the other one or two major constituents in the clause.

This hypothesis was tested using on-line narrations of two videos. I described the experiment and then analyzed the texts produced. The results of the experiment upheld my hypothesis in 93.5% to 100% of the clauses. Thus, for Cheyenne, the major constituent which is most newsworthy comes first in linear relationship to the other one or two major constituents in that clause, whether that constituent be the subject, object, or verb of the clause.

Appendix A
Cumulative Referential Density in Cheyenne

This appendix demonstrates the computation of cumulative referential density on a paragraph from *Bear Tepee* by Jeanette Howlingcrane (Leman 1980:13.1–7). References to the 'children' are underlined and references to the 'red paint' are bold. ('Red paint' is animate in Cheyenne and is thus translated as 'him' in sentences 4 and 5.)

(68)   1. <u>é-h-måsó-evo'sóe-hoon-o</u>   <u>ka'éškóneh-o</u>
           <u>3</u>-PST-sudden-play-PRET-<u>PL</u>   <u>child-PL</u>
           Children were playing.

   2. <u>é</u>-'-ŏhke-**pa'k-óma'e**-nené-sest-<u>o</u>   heše'ke-va
       <u>3</u>-PST-HABIT-**mound-ground**-make-PRET-<u>PL</u>   dirt-OBL
       They would make mounds in the dirt.

   3. tsé'tóhe **ma'etomo**
       this^AN **red^paint**
       "This is red paint,"

   4. <u>é</u>-'-ŏhkě-het-ó-**vŏ**-sest-**o**
       <u>3</u>-PST-HABIT-say-DIR-**3PL**-ATTR-**OBV**
       they would call to him.

5. *nėhe'še*
   then

   é-s-ta-ohke-osáanė-hé-mone-n-o-vȯ-sest-o
   3-PST-away-HABIT-commence-INT-choose-AN-DIR-3PL-ATTR-**OBV**
   Then they would choose him.

6. *é-x-ho-háe-nócné-sest-o*   *ka'ėskóneh-o*
   3-PST-very-many-be-ATTR-PL   child-PL
   There were lots of children.

7. *é-'-óhke-osáanė-hé-nomáhtse-n-ó-vȯ-sest-o*
   3-PST-HABIT-commence-INT-steal-INAN-DIR-3PL-ATTR-**OBV**

   néhe   *ma'etomon-o*
   the^AN   red^paint-OBV
   They would steal that red paint.

The table in (69) shows the computation of cumulative referential density (CRD) within this paragraph. CRD computation is outlined in example (29). An X in a column in (69) indicates that the participant is referenced in that clause. To calculate the CRD of a participant at a particular clause, add up the number of Xs in that participant's column up to and including that clause (total cumulative references) and divide the sum by the number of clauses up to that point in the paragraph (total cumulative clauses). For example, to calculate the CRD for the children in clause 4, add up the Xs in clauses 1–4 for a total of 3, and and divide by 4 with the results that the children's CRD at clause 4 is 0.75. For each clause, the most thematic participant is listed first in the final column, followed by the next most thematic. In clauses 3, 4, and 5 the children (C) and red paint (R) are equally thematic (=) because the CRD of each

Cumulative Referential Density in Cheyenne

is the same. In the other clauses the children are more thematic (>) than red paint because their CRD is larger.

(69) Computation of cumulative referential density (CRD)

Clause #	Children (C)	CRD	Red paint (R)	CRD	Thematic rank by clause
1	X	1.00		0.00	C>R
2	X	1.00	X	0.50	C>R
3		0.66	X	0.66	C=R
4	X	0.75	X	0.75	C=R
5	X	0.80	X	0.80	C=R
6	X	0.83		0.66	C>R
7	X	0.86	X	0.71	C>R

Appendix B
Diary of Video Experiment Process

As part of my preparation for the video experiment, I read *The Pear Stories*, edited by Wallace Chafe (1980). I was as much interested in the process as the results and was fascinated by the descriptions of the experiment. I decided to keep a diary of my video experiment and include it here.

I live in Hardin, Montana, 40 miles west of Busby where the video experiment was conducted. Busby is one of four towns on the Northern Cheyenne Indian reservation.

September 30 I visited with EA in Busby for a while then explained my experiment to her and asked for her help as a listener.

October 2 I went to Busby to ask GO to be a listener. I didn't find her.

October 4 I went to Busby again to see GO. After visiting with her, I explained the experiment to her and asked for her help as a listener. She agreed and volunteered to enlist two other listeners. We planned to demonstrate the experiment after an evening church service but it did not work out.

October 9 I went to visit GO again to see when we could work together. We agreed to get together on Monday the fifteenth. GO told me that one potential listener had just gotten a job.

From GO's, I went to see EA at work. We visited over lunch. I explained the experiment to her and she decided to help. I agreed to pick her up from work at 3:30 p.m. on Monday.

I decided to ask LF to be a listener. We arranged to meet at her house after her work was over on Monday at 4 p.m.

October 15 When I went to pick up EA at work, we visited awhile with EK. She told me that GO had asked her (EK) if I had been by to see her. She was wondering what I wanted and so I explained the experiment to her briefly. She seemed mildly interested.

EA and I went to LF's and waited for her to get off work. When she did, we went inside with my small black and white TV, VCR, and tape recorder. I explained the experiment to LF and EA. Then, I demonstrated to them in English an on-line narration of a video provided by Tomlin, each one watching a segment as I described it to the other. Then, I asked if they would be willing to demonstrate the procedure to the potential speakers. They agreed and practiced. First LF described *Fetch 1* to EA. GO arrived during LF's narration. Then EA described Fetch I to LF while GO observed. Then GO described *Fetch I* to LF. We then listened to the tape of their on-line narrations. They all agreed GO's was the best. We enjoyed the time of listening together. We agreed to meet the next day to begin conducting the experiment.

October 16 I picked EA up at work and we waited for LF. GO joined us at 4:30. We decided to ask TR for his help.

I explained the experiment to TR. He agreed to watch a demonstration. LF narrated the *Fetch 1* video to GO. Then TR narrated *Fetch 2* to GO. TR sat at a table with the equipment on it, EA sat behind him on a couch, while LF and GO sat on a couch that was parallel to the table. TR narrated the *Chicken* video three times. He did not seem to interact with or be influenced at all by the listeners while he was narrating the video. I think he would have told the stories the same way without the ladies there to listen. The ladies were interested in how TR narrated the stories, since he is an eloquent speaker. I noticed that on the third telling TR spoke a bit ahead of the video sequence anticipating what was to come, since he knew the story well by then.

October 17 I picked EA up at the usual time at AL's house. EK was there and I thought we might get her to be a speaker. I described to both AL and EK what the project entailed. We talked about it with EA. There was some discussion as to specific words that might be needed in narrating the video, especially words for tools of various sorts. We decided to wait until another time.

We went to LF's. Since she was not home, we left a note for her so she could find us at my office. I set the equipment up in the office. After

Diary of Video Experiment Process 85

awhile GO came in and a little later LF arrived. It turned out that the two potential speakers were unable to work with us. We agreed to meet next week.

October 25 LF took the day off from work. GO, LF, and I went to AL's house where EA was working. LF talked to AL a bit then told me to get the equipment. I set it up. GO demonstrated what we wanted with *Fetch 1*. AL agreed to help us. She practiced on *Fetch 1* then narrated the *Chicken* video. LF sat in the listener position; GO was where she could see the TV and in view of AL. About half way through EK walked in wondering what was going on at her sister's house. She watched AL finish narrating the *Chicken* video. I decided to ask her if she would help out too, before she saw the whole video. So LF went into the living room with AL, GO stayed in the kitchen, and EK practiced on *Fetch 1*. Then she went on to narrate *Chicken*. She didn't seem to need a listener. She narrated the *Chicken* video twice more before AL did it two more times. We visited awhile longer before leaving.

Although the listeners have not functioned as a 'naive' audience for each telling of the video, they provided moral support to the speaker initially by telling how they have each done the task, by demonstrating the task, and by being an encouragement while the speaker practices. The speaker is so intent on the video that (s)he is not paying attention to the audience. At this point I have gotten three speakers to give three on-line narrations of the *Chicken* video. With the amount of material generated by these narrations and the amount of time it will take to transcribe the material, I will have to limit the number of narrators.

November 14 I asked IR if she would be willing to help me with my experiment. We agreed to work at my office. After visiting awhile, I demonstrated on-line narration in English using the *Fetch 1* video. There were no other Cheyenne speakers present. IR then narrated the *Fetch 1* video twice before she felt comfortable enough to narrate the *Chicken* video. She then narrated the *Chicken* video three times. Before she left, we visited some more as we shared some donuts that she brought. I decided that with IR's narration, I now had enough data.

Appendix C
Samples of Cheyenne Texts

(70) *The Bear, the Coyote, and the Skunk* by Jeannette Howlingcrane (adapted from Leman 1980:27)

1. né-tå-hóhta'haov-åtse
   2-away-story^tell-1
   I'll tell you a story.

2. náhkohe   é-s-ta-ame-néhe-ohtsé-'ta-no-ho   meo'o
   bear   3-PST-away-along-follow-go-INAN-INAN-PRET   path
   A bear was following along a path.

3. hápó'e   nåháóhe   ó'kȯhome
   likewise   there   coyote

   mó-h-nėh-néhe-ohtsé-'tȯ-hé-he
   DUB-PST-toward-follow-go-INAN-NEG-NEG
   Likewise there a coyote was following it.

4. nėhe'še   é-s-too'e'ov-åhtsé-hoon-o
   then   3-PST-meet-RECIP-PRET-PL
   Then they met.

5. náhkohe   é-s-ta-tsė-het-ó-hoon-o   ó'kȯhomeh-o
   bear   3-PST-away-CATAPH-say-DIR-PRET-OBV   coyote-OBV
   The bear said to the coyote,

87

6. *no'hé-hně-stse*
   aside-walk-IMP
   "Move aside!"

7. *hé'tóhe   na-meo'o   é-x-het-ó-hoon-o*
   this^INAN   1PS-path   3-PST-say-DIR-PRET-OBV
   This is my path," he told him.

8. *hová'ǎháne   hápó'e   no'hé-hně-stse*
   no   likewise   aside-walk-IMP
   "No, likewise you move aside!"

9. *hé'tóhe   na-meo'o   é-x-het-ae-hoon-o*
   this^INAN   1PS-path   3-PST-say-INV-PRET-OBV
   This is my path," he told him.

10. *tsé-x-he'éše-óo'evot-åhtsé-vǒse   é-x-he'ke-mé'ě-hné-hoo'o*
    CJT-PST-while-argue-RECIP-3PL   3-PST-slow-appear-walk-PRET

    xao'o
    skunk
    While they were arguing, a skunk slowly appeared.

11. *háhtome*
    scram^IMP
    "Scram!"

12. *hé'tóhe   na-meo'o   é-x-het-ó-hoon-o*
    this^INAN   1PS-PATH   3-PST-say-DIR-PRET-OBV
    This is my path," he told them.

13. *é-x-he'ke-néma e-voněhné-hoo'o*
    3-PST-slowly-around-crawl-PRET
    He slowly turned around.

14. *é-x-he'kě-hešě-hosó-hně-hoo'o*
    3-PST-slowly-thus-backward-walk-PRET
    He slowly backed up.

Samples of Cheyenne Texts

15. *tsé-h-vóo-m-o-vôse*　　　*é-s-ta-néšê-he'név-o'åhéotsé-hoon-o*
    CJT-PST-see-AN-DIR-3PL　3-PST-away-two-spread-run-PRET-PL
    When they saw him, they took off in different directions.

16. *é-s-sáa-nåha'-óo-m-é-he-sest-o*　　　*tósa'e*
    3-PST-NEG-catch-see-AN-PSV-NEG-ATTR-PL　where

    tsé-heše-ase-ta'xé-vôse
    CJT-thus-off-spring-3PL
    They were not seen there where they took off to.

(71) *Fetch Story*, first telling by IR

1. *é-ta-ame-ohtsé-hoo'o*　　*hetane*
   3-away-along-go-PRET　　man
   A man is going along.

2. *oeškeso*　*é-ne'-amê-hné-hoo'o*
   dog　　　3-toward-along-walk-PRET
   A dog is walking along.

3. *é-ta-nó'êse-ka'a'xé-n-ô-hoon-o*　　　*ho'honaa'-o*
   3-away-over-jump-AN-DIR-PRET-OBV　rock-OBV
   He jumped over a rock.

4. *naa　hetane　é-tå-hóse-ame-ohtsé-hoo'o*
   and　man　　3-away-again-along-go-PRET
   And the man started going along again.

5. *oeškeso　é-s-ta-ame-nóhtsêhót-ô-hoon-o*　　　*hetan-óho*
   dog　　　3-PST-away-along-approach-DIR-PRET-OBV　man-OBV
   The dog approached the man.

6. *naa　hetane　é-s-ta-asê-ta'ham-ó-hoon-o*　　　*hohtsemon-o*
   and　man　　3-PST-away-off-throw-DIR-PRET-OBV　ball-OBV
   And the man throws a ball.

7. *naa　oeškeso　é-s-ta-néhe-ohé-'tov-ó-hoon-o*
   and　dog　　　3-PST-away-follow-move-AN-DIR-PRET-OBV
   And the dog chased it (ball is AN).

8. naa   néhe   oeškeso   é-s-tå-hóxove-ka'a'xe-sėstse
   and   the^AN   dog   3-PST-away-across-jump-ATTR

   tsé-'-ame-'sevo-tse   mahpe
   CJT-LOC-along-flow-OBV   water
   And the dog jumped across a stream.

9. é-ta-ase-néhe-ohé-'tov-ó-ho   hohtsemon-o
   3-away-off-follow-move-AN-DIR-OBV   ball-OBV
   He chased the ball.

10. naa   é-s-ta-évå-hósė-hóxove-ka'a'xe-sėstse   måhpe-va
    and   3-PST-away-back-again-across-jump-PRET   water-OBL
    And he jumped across the stream again.

11. naa   é-s-ta-évå-hósė-tšė-heše-méohé-hoo'o
    and   3-PST-away-back-again-CATAPH-thus-run-PRET

    hetan-óho   tsé-h-née-tsė-se
    man-OBV   where-LOC-stand-OBV-3
    And he ran back to where the man was standing.

12. é-s-tå-hóse-ka'a'xe-sėstse
    3-PST-away-again-jump-PRET
    He jumped again.

13. é-tå-hóse-ka'a'xé-n-ȯ-hoon-o   ho'honaa'-o
    3-away-again-jump-AN-DIR-PRET-OBV rock-OBV
    He jumped over the rock.

References

Beekman, John and John Callow. 1974. Translating the Word of God. Grand Rapids: Zondervan.

Bloomfield, Leonard. 1946. Algonquian. In Cornelius Osgood (ed.), Linguistic structures of native America, 85–129. Viking Fund Publications in Anthropology 6.

Callow, Kathleen. 1974. Discourse considerations in translating the Word of God. Grand Rapids: Zondervan.

Chafe, Wallace. 1974. Language and consciousness. Language 50:111–33.

———. 1976. Givenness, contrastiveness, definiteness, subjects, topics and point of view. In Charles N. Li (ed.), Subject and topic, 25–55. New York: Academic Press.

———, ed. 1980. The pear stories: Cognitive, cultural, and linguistic aspects of narrative production. Norwood, N.J.: Ablex Publishing.

———. 1987. Cognitive constraints on information flow. In Russell S. Tomlin (ed.), Coherence and grounding in discourse, 21–51. Amsterdam: John Benjamins.

Chomsky, Noam. 1965. Aspects of the theory of syntax. Cambridge: MIT Press.

Christopherson, P. 1939. The articles: A study of their theory and use in English. Copenhagen: Einar Munksgaard.

Cruse, D. A. 1973. Some thoughts on agentivity. Journal of Linguistics 9:11–23.

DeLancey, Scott. 1984. Notes on agentivity and causation. Studies in Language 8:181–213.

———. 1985. Agentivity and syntax. Papers from the Parasession on causatives and agentivity. Twenty-first Regional Meetings of the Chicago Linguistic Society, 25–27 April, 1985, 1–12. Chicago: University of Chicago.
Dik, Simon C. 1980. Studies in functional grammar. New York: Academic Press.
Dixon, R. M. W. 1994. Ergativity. Cambridge: Cambridge University Press.
Fillmore, Charles. 1968. The case for case. In E. Bach (ed.), Universals in linguistic theory, 1–90. New York: Holt, Rhinehart, and Winston.
———. 1971. Types of lexical information. In Danny D. Steinberg and Leon A. Jakobovits (eds.), Semantics: An interdisciplinary reader in philosophy, linguistics, and psychology, 370–92. Cambridge: Cambridge University Press.
———. 1977. Topics in lexical semantics. In Roger W. Cole (ed), Current issues in linguistic theory, 76–138. Bloomington: Indiana University Press.
Foley, William A. and Robert D. Van Valin. 1984. Functional syntax and univeral grammar. New York: Cambridge University Press.
Frishberg, Nancy. 1972. Navajo object markers and the great chain of being. In J. Kimbell (ed.), Syntax and semantics 1, 259–66. New York: Seminar Press.
Gernsbacher, Morton and David Hargreaves. 1992. The privilege of primacy: Experimental data and cognitive explanations. In Doris L. Payne (ed), Pragmatics of word order flexibility, 83–116. Amsterdam: John Benjamins.
Givón, Talmy. 1979. On understanding grammar. New York: Academic Press.
———. 1983. Topic continuity in discourse: Introduction. In Talmy Givón (ed.), Topic continuity in discourse: Quantified cross-language studies 1–41. Typological studies in language 3. Amsterdam: John Benjamins.
———. 1984. Syntax: A functional-typological introduction 1. Amsterdam: John Benjamins.
———. 1991. Serial verbs and mental reality of 'event': Grammatical vs. cognitive packaging. In Elizabeth Traugott and Brend Heine (eds), Approaches to grammaticalization, 81–127. Typological studies in language 19. Amsterdam: John Benjamins.
Goddard, Ives. 1990. Aspect of the topic structure of Fox narratives: Proximate shifts and the use of overt and inflectional NPs. International Journal of American Linguistics 56(3):317–40.
Grimes, Joseph. 1975. The thread of discourse. The Hague: Mouton.
Gruber, Jeffrey S. 1967. Look and see. Language 43:937–47.

References

Hale, Kenneth. 1973. A note on subject-object inversion in Navajo. In Braj B. Kachru, Robert B. Lees, Yakov Malkiel, Angelina Pietrangeli, and Sol Saporta (eds), Issues in linguistics: Papers in honor of Henry and Renee Kahane, 300–309. Champaign: University of Illinois Press.

Halliday, M. A. K. 1967. Some aspects of the thematic organization of the English clause. Memorandum RM-5224-PR. Santa Monica, Calif.: Rand Corporation.

——— and R. Hasan. 1976. Cohesion in English. London: Longman.

Haviland, Susan and Herbert Clark. 1974. What's new? Acquiring new information as a process in comprehension. JVLVB 13:512–21.

Hawkinson, A. and Larry Hyman. 1974. Hierarchies of natural topic in Shona. Studies in African Linguistics 5:147–70.

Hayashi, Larry. 1990. Event perception and clausal conjunctions. University of Oregon. ms.

Hinds, John. 1979. Organizational patterns in discourse. In Talmy Givón (ed.), Syntax and semantics, 135–57. New York: Academic Press.

Jones, Linda Kay. 1977. Theme in English expository discourse. Edward Sapir Monograph Series in Language, Culture, and Cognition 2. Lake Bluff, Ill.: Jupiter Press.

Keenan, Edward L. 1976. Toward a universal definition of subject. In Charles N. Li (ed.), Subject and topic, 303–34. New York: Academic Press.

Kuno, Susumu. 1972. Functional sentence perspective: A case study from Japanese and English. Linguistic Inquiry 3:269–320.

———. 1978. Generative discourse analysis in America. In W. Dressler (ed.), Current trends in text linguistics, 275–94. Berlin: De Gruyter.

Larsen, Iver. 1991a. Boundary features. Notes on Translation 5(1):48–54. Dallas: Summer Institute of Linguistics.

———. 1991b. Word order and relative prominence in New Testament Greek. Notes on Translation 5(1):29–34. Dallas: Summer Institute of Linguistics.

Leman, Wayne. 1979. Cheyenne grammar notes. Lame Deer, Mont.: Northern Cheyenne Bilingual Education Program.

———, ed. 1980. Cheyenne texts. Eastlake, Col.: Summer Institute of Linguistics.

———. 1981. Cheyenne pitch rules. International Journal of American Linguistics 47:283–309.

———. 1985. The discourse functions of Cheyenne demonstratives. University of Oregon. ms.

———, ed. 1987. Náévåhóó'ôhtséme/We are going back home (Cheyenne history and stories). Algonquian and Iroquoian Linguistics 4. Winnipeg.

Longacre, Robert E. 1970. Philippine languages: Discourse, paragraph and sentence structure. 1. Summer Institute of Linguistics Publications in Linguistics and Related Fields 21. Santa Ana, Calif.

———. 1979. The paragraph as a grammatical unit. In Talmy Givón (ed.), Syntax and semantics, 115–34. New York: Academic Press.

———. 1983. The grammar of discourse. New York: Plenum Press.

Lord, John B. 1964. The paragraph, structure and style. New York: Holt, Rinehart, and Winston.

Lyons, John. 1968. Introduction to theoretical linguistics. Cambridge: Cambridge University Press.

MacWhinney, Brian. 1977. Starting points. Language 53:152–68.

Mathesius, V. 1939. O tak zvaném aktuálním lenění větném [On the so-called actual bipartition of the sentence]. SaS 5:171–74.

———. 1942. e a sloh [Language and style]. In tení o jazyce a poezii, Praha 13–102.

Mithun, Marianne. 1987. Is basic word order universal? In Russell S. Tomlin (ed.), Coherence and grounding in discourse, 281–328. Amsterdam: John Benjamins.

Payne, Doris L. 1987. Information structuring in Papago narrative discourse. Language 63:783–804.

———. 1991. Verb initial languages and information order. University of Oregon. ms.

Pike, Kenneth L. and Evelyn G. Pike. 1982. Grammatical analysis. 2nd ed. Dallas: Summer Institute of Linguistics.

Postal, Paul. 1974. On raising. Cambridge: MIT Press.

Prince, Ellen. 1978. A comparison of wh-clefts and it-clefts in discourse. Language 54:883–906.

———. 1979. On the given-new distinction. In Paul Clyne, William F. Hanks, and Carol Haufbauer (eds.), Papers from the Fifteenth Regional Meeting of the Chicago Linguistic Society, 19–20 April, 1979, 267–78. Chicago: University of Chicago.

Ransom, Evelyn. 1977. Definiteness, animacy, and NP ordering. In Kenneth Whistler, Robert D. Van Valin, Chris Chiarello, Jeri J. Jaeger, Miriam Petruck, Henry Thompson, Ronya Javkin, and Anthony Woodbury (eds), Proceedings of the Third Annual Meeting of the Berkeley Linguistics Society, 19–21 February, 1977, 418–29. Berkeley: University of California.

Schwartz, A. 1974. The VP-constituent of SVO languages. In Luigi Heilmann (ed.), Proceedings of the Eleventh International Congress of Linguists, Bologna-Florence, Italy, 28 August–2 September, 1972, 619–37. Bologna: Il Mulino.

References

Silverstein, Michael. 1976. Hierarchy of features and ergativity. In Robert M. W. Dixon (ed.), Grammatical categories in Australian languages, 112–71. Canberra: Australian Institute of Aboriginal Studies.

Tomlin, Russell S. 1986. Basic constituent order: Functional principles. London: Croom Helm.

———. 1987. Linguistic reflections of cognitive events. In Russell S. Tomlin (ed.), Coherence and grounding in discourse, 455–79. Amsterdam: John Benjamins.

——— and Richard Rhodes. 1979. An introduction to information distribution in Ojibwa. In Paul R. Clyne, William F. Hanks, and Carol L. Hofbauer (eds), Papers from the Fifteenth Regional Meeting of the Chicago Linguistic Society, 307–21. Chicago: University of Chicago.

Warren, John, H. Williams, and Robert E. Shaw. 1985. Events and encounters as units of analysis for ecological psychology. In John Warren, H. Williams, and Robert E. Shaw (eds.), Persistence and change: Proceedings of the First International Conference on Event Perception, 1–27. Hillsdale, N.J.: Lawrence Erlbaum.

www.ingramcontent.com/pod-product-compliance
Lightning Source LLC
Chambersburg PA
CBHW070815250426
43672CB00030B/2744